THE BIG BOOK OF KNITTING

The Big Book of Knitting

Ursula von Wartburg

KESTREL BOOKS

To the children of the Workshop

KESTREL BOOKS
Published by Penguin Books Ltd
Harmondsworth, Middlesex, England

First published in the USA by Atheneum, New York, 1973
under the title The Workshop Book of Knitting

ISBN 0 7226 5083 3

Printed in Great Britain by Lowe & Brydone Ltd, Thetford, Norfolk

Filmset by Typesetting Services Ltd, Glasgow and Edinburgh

ACKNOWLEDGEMENTS

I would like to thank Devereux P. Wight for his constant help and encouragement. I would also like to thank Dieter Luft, William F. Pons, and Gene Bourne for their photographic contributions. The majority of drawings were done by Margrit Senn.

My appreciation goes out to my editor Jean Karl, whose enthusiasm and acceptance made this book possible.

INTRODUCTION

The Big Book of Knitting was inspired by the children in the workshop that I conduct in New York City. The children attend the workshop for a two-hour session once a week during the academic year.

The instructions contained in this book were constantly tested out with the children. Changes were made to ensure clarity. If you are a beginner I suggest that you start with the first project. The projects gradually become more involved as you progress. New knitting processes are explained at the end of each project.

The students responded to colours and different kinds of material with great enthusiasm. It is my hope that you will find the joy they had when knitting for yourself or for others.

Metric conversion table

1 cm	=	0·39 inch
2 cm	=	0·79 inch
3 cm	=	1·18 inches
4 cm	=	1·58 inches
5 cm	=	1·97 inches
6 cm	=	2·36 inches
7 cm	=	2·76 inches
8 cm	=	3·15 inches
9 cm	=	3·54 inches
10 cm	=	3·94 inches
1 metre	=	39·4 inches

CONTENTS

THE BIG
BOOK OF KNITTING

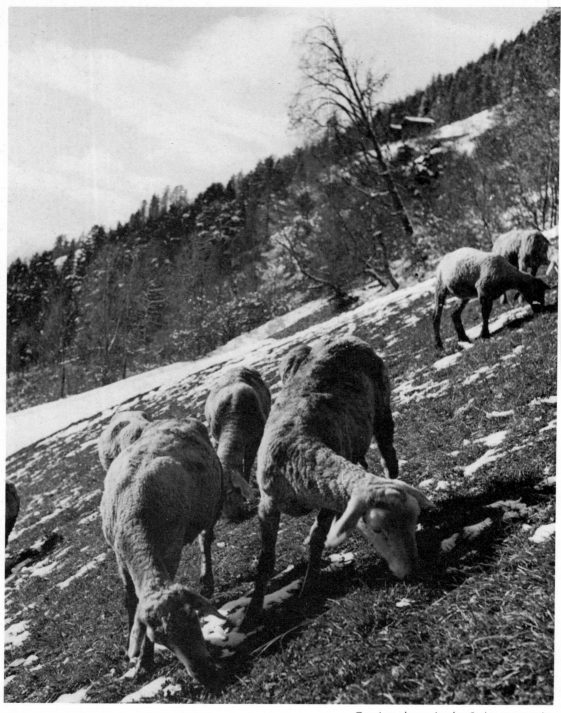

Grazing sheep in the Swiss mountains

MATERIALS AND TOOLS FOR KNITTING

Spinning wool by hand in southern Switzerland

Wool

Wool comes from the soft, curly hair that covers the bodies of sheep. It is sheared during the spring because in summer the animal is more comfortable without its bushy coat of hair. In the autumn the hair will have grown back to keep the sheep's body warm for winter.

The hair that has been cut off is brushed and combed to remove leaves and twigs. Then it is washed. The pieces of hair are spun (twisted together) into one long thread called yarn. This process is usually done by machine; but in some places it is still done by hand on a spinning-wheel. Hand-spun yarn has a quality all its own. It is uneven and bumpy in places, which gives it a unique charm not found in machine-made yarn.

Wool knitting-yarn is available in hundreds of colours and shades, and in different thicknesses, twists, and textures.

Claudia L., age 14

Different Kinds of Yarn

FIBRE	ORIGIN	CHARACTERISTICS
Wool	Fleece of sheep	Soft, resilient, warm.
Mohair	Hair of goats	Soft, lightweight, warm. Because mohair sheds, it is not recommended for baby clothing.
Angora	Hair of Angora rabbits	Fluffy, soft, warm. Sheds. Expensive.
Cotton	Cotton plant	Strong and durable. Absorbent. Not warm.
Linen	Flax plant	Strong and durable. Often mixed with cotton or silk. Has an attractive shine.
Nylon and Orlon	Chemical industry	Wears long, dries fast. Not as warm or absorbent as wool. Often combined with cotton or wool.

Cotton

LAUNDERING INSTRUCTIONS

Wash gently by hand in luke-
warm water with mild soap. Rinse
in cold water. Do not wring. For
coloured materials, add 2 tablespoons
of white vinegar to the final rinse.
Roll in a towel to remove excess water.
Place on a flat surface to dry,
shaping to proper size.

Machine-washable. Can withstand
strong soaps.

Carefully hand-launder or, better
still, dry-clean.

Machine-washable. Turn garment
inside out before washing. Pat
sweaters into shape on a flat
surface and leave to dry.

Cotton comes from a plant grown in
the southern part of the United States
and in other comparable areas of the
world. In April or May the seeds are
planted in rows in huge fields. They
grow into upright plants from 1 to 7
feet tall and branch out in all directions.

Cotton flower

The flowering season of the cotton plant
is during the summer. Only one or two
white flowers open each day, starting
at the bottom of the plant and up to
the top. The flowers wither after 24
hours, turning pink, then blue and finally
purple as they dry and fall off the plant.
The fluffy cotton fibre starts to grow
inside a protective cover called the *boll*.
It takes until autumn for the cotton to

5

mature. Then the boll pops open and exposes the fluffy, soft cotton, looking like snowballs and covering the field.

Cotton boll

Cotton is harvested by hand or machine, closely packed into large packages called *bales* and sold to textile mills. There the seeds and twigs are cleaned out, and the cotton is washed and spun into threads. The threads are used for weaving fabrics, knitting, crocheting, and many other purposes.

Cotton yarns are available in many colours and in a wide range of weights and textures. There are thin yarns for crocheting lace around handkerchiefs and embroidering, thick ones for pot-holders, strong ones for making canvas, and cord, and many other types.

6

How Yarn Is Sold

Knitting yarn is usually sold in balls, which are held together by a paper band. Save this band to be sure of getting the same yarn if you have to buy more; it contains important information such as:

Brand name
Amount of yarn in ounces or grams*
Thickness
Colour name and dye-lot number
Fibre content
Washing instructions

Most balls are ready for knitting. Look for the beginning of the yarn, which will be outside the ball. Some yarns, however, are sold in skeins, and must be re-wound into a ball before knitting. (See page 8.)

*1 ounce = 28·35 grams

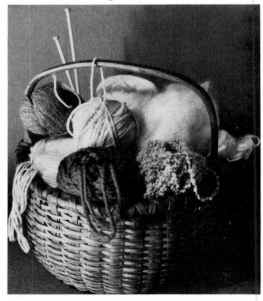

The Basic Weights of Yarn and the Needles to Use

KIND	THICKNESS	NEEDLE SIZE	USES
Baby yarn (2, 3 and 4 ply)	very thin	12–11	Baby clothes and any fine light and delicate knitting.
4 ply	thin	11–10	Socks, light pullovers, toys, children's clothing.
Double knitting	medium thick	10–7	Ski wear, blankets, toys, headbands, coat-hanger covers, needle-book cover, etc. *Good yarn for beginners.*
Chunky yarn; double double knitting	thick	6–3	Heavy blankets, house slippers, ski hat, etc.
Rug yarn	extra thick	2–00	Potholders, bath mats, shoulder bags, etc.

The ply indicates the number of spun threads that have been twisted together to form the yarn.

If you have a tendency to knit tightly use the next larger size needle than the one recommended and vice versa.

Suggestion: Just for fun, try knitting with unusual materials. For example you might want to show someone at school how to knit by using pencils for needles and shoelaces for yarn. When out in the country find two smooth sticks and try knitting with tall grasses and hay.

Catherine S., age 12

7

Winding Yarn

When winding is necessary,

1 Remove the paper band that holds the skein together.

2 Carefully unfold the skein and place it over the back of a chair, or have someone hold it for you. If the skein is divided in half, separate the 2 parts and wind them one at a time.

3 Cut the thin string or yarn that is tied around the yarn strands. Look for the yarn ends, which are knotted together around the skein. Cut open close to the knot. Use either end for the beginning.

4 To make sure you won't lose the wrapper that held the skein together, fold the wrapper and wind the yarn around it to form a ball.

Fannie I., age 8

Suggestion: Make a Surprise Ball for someone. Wind sweets and little trinkets into a knitting ball. The knitter will be delighted when the surprises fall out as the ball of yarn unwinds. (I remember with pleasure one my grandmother gave me when I was a child. As I knitted, much to my surprise, little notes to me fell out of the ball, and at the end there was a little silver charm.)

Knitting-Needles

Knitting-needles are made of either plastic or coated metal. The 2 basic types are single- and double-pointed and they come in a variety of thicknesses and several lengths.

Single-pointed needles are sold in pairs. They have a knob at one end and come in 3 lengths—short (25·5 cm), medium (30·5 cm), and long (35·5 cm).

Katherine M., age 13

Double-pointed needles come in sets of 4 and are usually 17·7 cm long. Needle sizes go from 00 to 14, 00 being the thickest.

Shivan S., age 8

Paper-clip. Hang a paper-clip onto the knitting yarn and slide it next to the last knitted stitch as a marker.

Tapestry needles, sizes 18 and 20, for sewing together knitted pieces and sewing in yarn ends. It is easy to thread these needles because they have large eyes. They also have dull points.

Crochet hook, which is a straight needle with a hook at one end, for crocheting and for picking up dropped stitches. Use size 4.50 for medium-thick yarn and size 2.50 for finer yarn.

Safety pins, small and medium sizes, for weaving drawstrings into knitting.

Handkerchief, man's size, for wrapping delicate knitting.

Other Helpful Tools

Scissors for cutting yarn, paper, and cardboard.

Ruler for measuring knitting and paper.

Pencil. Besides writing with it, you will use it in making a twisted cord.

Notebook for keeping knitting patterns, designs, and ideas; also for sketching projects.

Claudia L., age 14

Cable needle for holding stitches when knitting cable patterns. (You can also use a wooden match or any short double-pointed needle for a cable needle.)

Stitch holder, which looks like a large safety-pin, for holding stitches. (You can also thread stitches onto a piece of yarn to hold them.)

Row knitting

WHAT YOU NEED TO KNOW

The Knit Stitch

Catherine S., age 12

Row Knitting

Two needles are used in row knitting. You hold the needle with the work on it in your left hand and knit the work off onto the empty needle in your right hand. When you have knitted all the stitches from one needle onto the other you have knitted 1 row. To continue knitting, go back and forth, turning the work around at the end of each row.

The knit stitch is the basic stitch in knitting. You see knit stitches all over the stocking-stitch pattern. Most often pullovers and feet of socks are knitted in this pattern. The knit stitch has a flat, even surface. If you inspect a single stitch you will find it looks like the letter V. The reverse side of a knit stitch is bumpy and is called a purl stitch (see page 12).

Alexandra S., age 11

Make it a habit to finish the row before putting aside your knitting. But, if you had to put down your knitting before finishing the row, make sure you pick it up again the right way. The needle holding the last knitted stitch goes in your right hand.

Electra R., age 10

The Garter-Stitch Pattern

The garter-stitch pattern consists of ridges that run across the knitting parallel to the needle. The ridges are purl stitches and the valleys in between are knit stitches. The ridges come about because the rows of knit stitches on the inside are rows of purl stitches on the outside. The pattern looks the same on both sides.

The Purl Stitch

The second most important stitch is the purl stitch. You can see it on the inside of your socks' feet. It is almost never used alone as a pattern stitch; but combined with the knit stitch it forms interesting patterns. The reverse side of a purl stitch is a knit stitch (see page 11).

KNITTING INSTRUCTIONS

To knit garter-stitch you only have to know how to do the knit stitch, and then knit it continuously on both sides of your work. By knitting 2 rows, you make 1 garter-stitch row.
Always count garter-stitch rows on the outside of the knitting.

12

How to Tell the Outside from the Inside

The outside of the knitting is the side you will want to show.

When you cast on stitches, a piece of the measured length of yarn is left over. If this leftover piece is on your left, you are looking at the outside of the knitting. If the piece of yarn is on your right, you are looking at the inside of the knitting.

You can also tell the difference between outside and inside by the cast-on edge. The inside of the cast-on edge is bumpy compared with the outside.

Inside

Outside

How to Take Care of Your Knitting

1 Store your knitting tools and materials in a box such as a shoe box, and keep light-coloured knitting wrapped up in a handkerchief or teatowel.

2 Don't let the ball of yarn roll around on the floor while you are knitting.

3 Wash your hands with soap and water before starting to knit. Also wash them if they become moist and sticky while knitting.

4 Do not rest your elbows on a table while knitting. Sit back in your chair and relax.

5 Make it a habit to finish the row or round before putting your knitting away.

Catherine S., age 12

6 When you put your knitting away, place one needle over the other and wrap yarn around the needles so the stitches won't slide off.

7 Make your workplace a happy place to be. Tidy up around you. Work with good light on your knitting.

How to Make a Slipknot

It is important to know how to make a slipknot because it is the basis of knitting. The first stitch you put on the needle *is* a slipknot, and the following stitches are similar to it although made a little differently.

1 Cut a piece of yarn about 2 arms' length and straighten it out in front of you on a table.

2 Make a small loop in the yarn by crossing one side over the other.

3 Take the piece of yarn that crosses in front and bring it under and across the back of the loop.

4 Pull through the loop the part of the yarn that is crossing at the back, while lightly holding both strands with the other hand. Tighten the slip-knot.

5 Pull each yarn end to see which one makes the loop smaller. Pull on the loop if you want to make it bigger.

Suggestion: To practise making slip-knots, make them an inch or so apart. Place sweets, flowers or small bundles of different-coloured yarn strands in the loops and make a necklace or bracelet. Use a longer piece of yarn if you want to make a belt or headband.

15

Casting On for Beginners

To start your knitting you must know how to cast on stitches. In this process you make slipknots out of 2 strands of yarn and place them on a knitting needle.

1 Find the beginning of the yarn (see page 6). Make a slipknot (see page 14) 1 arm's length from the beginning. Do not cut the yarn.

2 Put the slipknot onto a knitting needle and tighten it loosely around the needle. This is your first stitch. Hold the needle in your right hand like holding a handle.

3 About 1·2 cm from the first stitch make a small loop in the measured length of yarn *with the free end crossing over in front*. Hold the loop in your left hand.

4 Bring the yarn coming from the ball across the back of the loop.

5 Pass the needle, top to bottom, under the yarn that crosses at the back of the loop. Pull the yarn up through the loop and onto the needle. This is the second stitch.

6 Tighten the second stitch by pulling on both strands under the needle.

7 Repeat steps 3 to 6 for as many stitches as you need to cast on.

8 Cut the measured piece of yarn, leaving about 7·5 cm.

Casting On a Faster Way

(*The Thumb Method*)

Rule: 1 needle's length of yarn makes about 10 stitches. Add an extra needle's length for good measure.

1 Measure out the needed length of yarn and make a slipknot at that point. Put the slipknot on the needle 2·5 cm from the tip and tighten it loosely around the needle.

2 Now place your right hand over the needle with your thumb on the stitch and hold the needle in your hand the way you would hold a handle.

4 Push the strands apart with your left index finger and thumb, the measured strand against your thumb. Spread the 2 fingers as far apart as you can.

3 Hold the 2 yarn strands in your left hand, with the last 3 fingers closing over them.

5 Bring the needle over to the thumb so that the yarn crosses and makes a loop.

6 Bring the tip of the needle up through the loop on your thumb.

7 With the tip of the needle catch the other strand and pull it through the loop.

Important: Be sure you don't tighten the stitches too much; they must slide easily on the needle. If your stitches keep coming out too tight, try casting on over 2 needles and then pulling one needle out.

8 Pull your thumb out of the loop and put it under the needle, behind the measured strand. Now swing your thumb out against the strand, tightening the stitch. At the same time you will be forming a new loop around your thumb.

9 Repeat steps 5 to 8 for the number of stitches you need.

PROJECT 1

KNITTING A BOOKMARK

and Learning How to Do the Knit Stitch

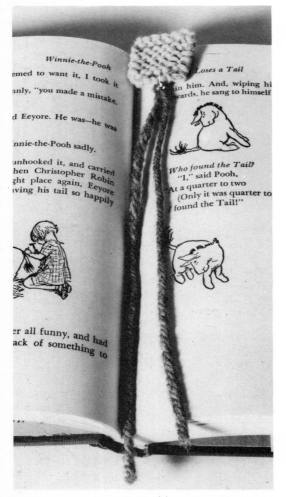

Knitted by Janine A., age 12

MATERIAL NEEDED

Small amount of double knitting yarn.
1 pair of short knitting-needles, size 9.

WORK METHOD

Casting on
Row knitting
Casting off (See page 24.)

PATTERN STITCH

Garter stitch (See page 12.)

KNITTING INSTRUCTIONS

1 Cast on 6 stitches.

2 Get ready to knit:

a Hold the needle with the cast-on stitches in your right hand, the way you would hold a handle.

b Spread apart the fingers of your left hand and loosely wind the yarn from the ball over your little finger, in across the middle and ring fingers, then out and twice around the index finger.

20

c Practise pulling the yarn through your fingers. If the yarn does not slide easily, wash your hands with soap and water. Try again.

d Switch the needle over into your left hand. Hold it near the tip with your last 3 fingers and thumb closed over the stitches.

e Check the position of each finger. *Index finger* is up. Its job is to hold the yarn. *Middle finger* and *thumb* must hold the stitch that is nearest to the tip of the needle. This keeps it from slipping off. *Ring finger* and *little finger* help to hold the needle.

f The empty needle is held near the tip with all fingers of the right hand, as you would hold a handle.

3 Learning how to do the knit stitch:

a Put the tip of the right-hand needle between the first 2 stitches and up through the bottom of the first stitch, front to back.

b Pass the needle over the strand of yarn coming from your left index finger. Bring the needle around the yarn. Hold the yarn with your index finger so it won't slip off.

c Bring the needle with the yarn on it back through the stitch.

d Slide off the stitch on the left-hand needle and tighten the new stitch on the right-hand needle.

e Repeat steps a to d to the end of the row.

22

It helps to count rhythmically 1-2-3-4 as you do each step, or to say to yourself at each step:

a through the stitch
b yarn around
c bring yarn back
d slide off old stitch

4 How to change needles to start a new row:

a Bring the yarn coming from the left index finger under the needle, then change the needle, with the tip away from you, over into your left hand again. Make sure the yarn is under and behind the needle.

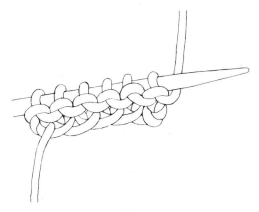

b Take the empty needle in your right hand.

5 Knit the second row. Work slowly and carefully.

6 Knit until you have 5 garter-stitch rows (or 10 rows of knitting altogether). Compare your work with the photograph.

7 Cast off. (See page 24.)

FINISHING INSTRUCTIONS

Sew in yarn ends.

How to Cast Off

This is a way of finishing off knitting. It makes a firm edge that won't unravel. As a rule cast off in your pattern stitch and on the outside of the knitting.

KNITTING INSTRUCTIONS

Be sure to knit each stitch loosely.

1 Knit the first 2 stitches.

2 With the point of the left-hand needle loosen the back stitch, then pull the front stitch through it and let the back stitch go.

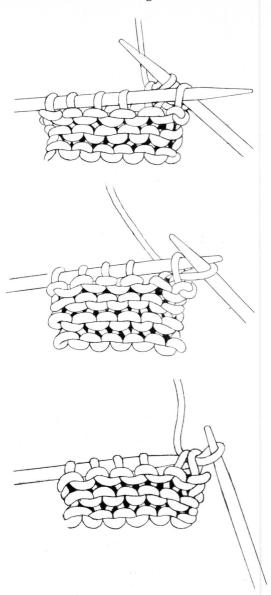

3 Knit another stitch onto the right-hand needle.

24

4 Again loosen the back stitch and pull the front stitch through it, letting the back stitch go (as in step 2).

5 Repeat steps 3 and 4 to end of row. You will have 1 stitch left over at the end.

6 Cut the yarn about 7·5 cm from the stitch. Bring the yarn up through the stitch. Remove the needle and pull the stitch tight.

HEADBAND

You can knit a headband in a few hours. Make a narrow one for school on 6 stitches and a wide one to keep your ears warm for winter on 16 stitches.

Knitted by Katie D., age 9

MATERIAL NEEDED

1 small ball of double knitting yarn
1 pair of short knitting-needles, size 9
(See page 8.)
1 tapestry needle

WORK METHOD

Casting on
Row knitting
Edge stitch (See page 28.)
Casting off

PATTERN STITCH

Garter stitch

KNITTING INSTRUCTIONS

‡ This symbol means work edge stitch. See page 28 for instructions.

1 Cast on 6 stitches.

2 Knit all 6 stitches on the first row.

3‡ Knit until you have 3 garter-stitch rows. Be sure you always have 6 stitches on the needle.

4 Compare your knitting with the photograph. If it looks the same, continue; if not, unravel the knitting and start again. Work carefully to avoid making the following mistakes:

a dropping a stitch;

b forgetting to bring the needle with the yarn on it back through the stitch;

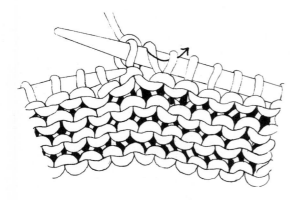

c splitting the yarn of the stitch with the point of the needle;

d inserting the right-hand needle through the row below instead of through the stitch on the needle;

5‡ Knit until you have a total of 36 garter-stitch rows.

6 Stretch the knitting lightly and try it around your head. If necessary knit a few more rows.

7‡ Cast off on the outside of the knitting. Leave 1 arm's length of yarn for sewing the headband together.

FINISHING INSTRUCTIONS

1 Sew the cast-on and cast-off edges together.

2 Sew in any yarn ends along the edge.

Edge Stitch

Edge stitch is firm and has a finished look. It is used in row knitting and is made with the first and last stitches of every row. If you find it difficult to do the edge stitch on the first row after casting on, however, it is all right to knit the very first stitch.

Susan S., age 12

KNITTING INSTRUCTIONS

‡Slip the first stitch on the row over to the empty needle without knitting it. Knit the last stitch on the row.

The symbol ‡ is used throughout the knitting instructions in this book to remind you to work edge stitch. Whenever you see the symbol ‡ before a step in the instructions, *slip the first stitch and knit the last stitch on the row.*

28

HANGER COVER

Another good project for practising the knit stitch is this cover for a wooden hanger. Knit covers in solid colours or in stripes. They make practical gifts and usually sell well at a bazaar.

MATERIAL NEEDED

1 small ball of double knitting yarn or small amounts of leftover yarn of same thickness in several colours for a striped cover
1 pair of short knitting-needles, size 9 (See page 8.)
1 straight wooden hanger
1 tapestry needle

WORK METHOD

Casting on
Row knitting
Edge stitch
Casting off
Joining yarn to change colours if making a striped cover

PATTERN STITCH

Garter stitch

Margot O., age 12

29

KNITTING INSTRUCTIONS

‡Edge stitch

1   Cast on 10 stitches.

2   Knit all 10 stitches on the first row.

3‡ Knit until you have 8 garter-stitch rows. Compare your knitting with the photograph. At this point tie a marker of different coloured yarn around the knitting yarn and slide it next to the last knitted stitch.

4‡ Knit until you have about 45 garter-stitch rows. Be sure you always have 10 stitches on the needle. Try to avoid mistakes.

5   Stretch your knitting lightly and hold it along the hanger to check the length. If necessary knit more rows to fit. See photograph. Finish knitting on an inside row.

6‡ Cast off. Leave 3 arms' lengths of yarn for sewing.

FINISHING INSTRUCTIONS

1   Fold the cast-on and cast-off edges in half and sew each edge together on the outside of the knitting.

2   If you knitted a striped cover, darn each coloured strand through knitting of the same colour.

3   Count the total number of garter-stitch rows and find the centre. Push the hanger hook through the centre.

4   Pull the ends over the hanger and sew together the edge-stitched edges at the bottom of the hanger.

How to Join Yarn and Change Colours

Join yarn to continue knitting when you come to the end of a ball or to create patterns with various colours and textures of yarn. There is no limit to the colour combinations and special effects. Collect leftover yarn and either sketch your colour arrangement or create a design as you knit. (See the sketches by Katherine M., age 10.)

KNITTING INSTRUCTIONS

Row Knitting

1 Work to the last stitch on the inside row.

2 Put the new yarn alongside the old one and knit the last stitch with both yarns. Drop the old yarn and cut it about 10 cm from the stitch.

3 Put the new yarn on your hand and continue to knit.

Treat the 2-yarn stitch as a single stitch by working both strands together. Make sure to start each new colour at the same edge.

Note: When changing colours in a scarf knitted in garter stitch, knit 1 stitch, purl 1 stitch on the first row with each new colour. This keeps the knitting looking the same on both sides.

Round Knitting

1 Work to the end of a round.

2 Tie the new and the old yarns together loosely right next to the last knitted stitch. The free ends of yarn must be at least 8 cm long.

3 Keep the knot on the inside of the knitting and continue knitting with the new yarn.

4 The knot will be undone and the ends sewn in when you are finishing the project. (See page 140.)

How to Use a Marker

A marker marks a specific place in your knitting. From that point, it is easy to count stitches or rows. A marker also lets you see immediately where you started increasing or decreasing, for instance, and can be most helpful in knitting complicated patterns such as cabling, where you have to repeat a certain process every so many rows.

A marker can be:

1 A piece of contrasting-coloured yarn either sewn into the knitting or tied around the knitting yarn and then moved next to the last knitted stitch.

2 A paper-clip or safety-pin.

How to Correct a Mistake

There are several ways to correct a mistake in your knitting. Choosing the right method depends on the pattern stitch and the position of the mistake.

ON THE NEEDLE

When there is a mistake in the row you are working on, you can take out or "undo" as many stitches as necessary without pulling out the needles. The work is held the same way it is when you are knitting.

1 Insert the tip of the left-hand needle through the front of the stitch below the last knitted one on the right-hand needle.

2 Slip the stitch off the right-hand needle and pull the yarn to undo it.

3 Repeat steps 1 and 2 until you have undone all the stitches you want; then rework the stitches.

IN THE KNITTING

When there is a mistake several rows below the needle:

1 For stocking stitch and ribbing patterns:

a Knit to the stitch directly above the mistake.

b Drop the stitch off the needle and undo it row by row until you get down to the mistake. This will form a "ladder", like a run in a stocking.

c With a crochet hook loop each rung of the ladder through the stitch below, moving from the bottom up. When the stitch is worked all the way back up to the needle, be sure to place it on the needle, facing in the same direction as the other stitches.

Note: Knit stitches are easier to pick up than purl stitches. To pick up purl stitches, turn the knitting around and do it from the other side.

2 For garter stitch and complicated patterns:

a Pull the needles out of the knitting.

b Pull on the yarn to unravel as much of the knitting as necessary, stopping at the end of a row.

c Hold the knitting in your left hand the way you would if you were knitting.

d Take the needle in your right hand and insert the point, back to front, through the stitch that is right under a loose stitch.

e Pull the yarn just enough to undo that loose stitch. Undoing this extra row helps you to get all the stitches correctly back onto the needle.

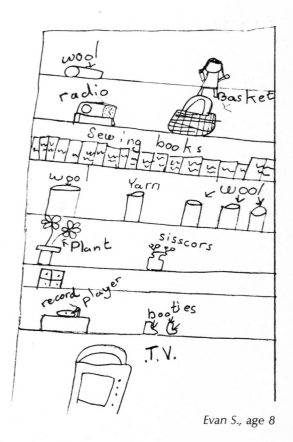

Evan S., age 8

35

NEEDLE BOOK

This is a most useful little project. The cover is knitted; the pages are made of felt. Keep your tapestry needles on one page, safety pins on another, then fine sewing needles and pins. Paper clips for knitting markers can be hooked on the inside of the cover. A needle book is handy when travelling. It makes a nice gift.

MATERIAL NEEDED

1 small ball of double knitting yarn or small amounts of leftover yarn of same thickness in several colours
1 pair of short knitting-needles, size 9 (See page 8.)
1 tapestry needle

WORK METHOD

Casting on
Row knitting
Edge stitch
Casting off
Joining yarn to change colours (optional)

PATTERN STITCH

Garter stitch

KNITTING INSTRUCTIONS

‡Edge stitch

A Knitting the cover from side to side:

1 Cast on 20 stitches.

2‡ Knit 34 garter-stitch rows.

3‡ Cast off.

Julie B., age 11

Knitted by Julie B., age 11

B Knitting the cover from bottom to top:

    1 Cast on 31 stitches.

    2‡ Knit 19 or 20 garter-stitch rows.

    3‡ Cast off.

FINISHING INSTRUCTIONS

1 Sew in all yarn ends on the inside. If you changed colours sew through knitting of the same colour.

2 Cut 6 pieces of yarn each one arm's length.

3 Sew 3 pieces together through the centre of the edge of the front and back covers. See illustration.

4 Bring the ends together and plait the three doubled strands. Tie knots at the ends.

5 Cut 2 double pages of felt slightly smaller than the cover.

6 Place the felt pieces against the inside of the cover.

7 Sew the pages to the cover.

Knitted by Jennifer M., age 10

INDOOR BALL

This is an ideal ball for playing with in the house. It is soft, lightweight, has a nice bounce and is almost noiseless. Wash it in warm water and mild soap, and rinse well. The ball takes a few days to dry.

MATERIAL NEEDED

Three 25-gram balls of double knitting yarn or small amounts of leftover yarn of same thickness in several colours
1 pair of short knitting-needles, size 9 (See page 8.)
Stuffing material (See page 54.)
1 tapestry needle

WORK METHOD

Casting on
Row knitting
Edge stitch
Joining yarns to change colours (optional)
Casting off

PATTERN STITCH

Garter stitch

MAKING THE INSIDE OF THE BALL

1 Cut a rag or torn nylon stockings into pieces.

2 Bunch the pieces into a ball and, if available, put a layer of synthetic fibre stuffing all around it.

3 Wind yarn around the ball to hold it together. See illustration. Ball has to be firm and well shaped.

Knitted by Caroline F., age 9

38

FINDING OUT HOW MANY STITCHES TO CAST ON

1 Measure the ball by putting a strip of paper around it tightly.

2 Half of this measurement is the casting-on width. You will knit a strip long enough to fit around the ball.

KNITTING THE COVER

‡Edge stitch

1 Cast on stitches equal to the width. Spread apart the cast-on stitches on the needle. See illustration.

2‡ Knit as many rows of garter stitch as needed to fit the knitting tightly around the ball.

3‡ Cast off. Leave 1 arm's length of yarn for sewing.

FINISHING INSTRUCTIONS

1 Sew cast-on and cast-off edges together to form a ring.

2 With tapestry needle, draw a piece of yarn through the edge-stitched edge on one side.

3 Pull together the opening. Bring the yarn through the stitches once more, pulling the opening completely closed.

4 Fold all yarn ends inside and place the ball in the cover.

5 Sew and pull together the other opening as in steps 2 and 3.

40

SCARF

This different-looking scarf is fun to knit and takes surprisingly little time because of the extra-long stitches. To make the long stitches, you will be using a ruler or strip of cardboard in place of a needle. You can vary the number of garter-stitch rows.

MATERIAL NEEDED

Nine 25-gram balls of double knitting yarn

1 pair of knitting-needles, size 6 (extra large)

One 30 cm ruler about 2·5 cm wide, or a strip of cardboard about the same shape.

WORK METHOD

Casting on
Row knitting
Edge stitch
Casting off

PATTERN STITCH

Garter stitch

KNITTING INSTRUCTIONS

‡Edge stitch

1   Cast on 36 stitches.

2‡ Knit until you have 10 garter-stitch rows.

3   Slip the first stitch, pull it up, and put it onto a ruler. See illustration. Knit each stitch and slip it onto the ruler for the entire row.

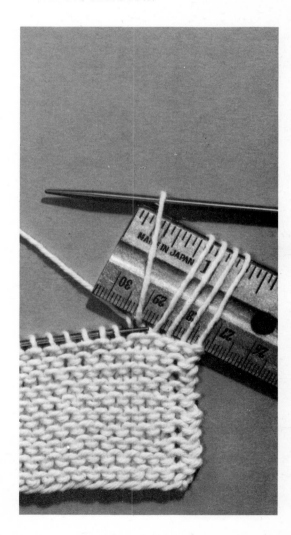

4 Knit the stitches off the ruler onto the needle. Pull on the needle after each stitch to keep the stitches the size of the ruler.

5 Count the stitches on the needle. There should be 36.

6‡ Knit 10 garter-stitch rows.

7 Repeat steps 3 to 5 until your scarf is as long as you want. End with 10 garter-stitch rows.

8‡ Cast off. Leave a half arm's length of yarn.

FINISHING INSTRUCTIONS

1 Sew in all yarn ends.

2 Add fringe. (See page 44.)

42

Knitted by Beatrice R., age 12

Knitted by Soledad A., age 9

Beatrice

Scarf

1st cast on 36

two different colors

3 means 3 garter rows and 2

3 2 3 2 3 2 3 means 2

garter rows

red + light purple

After I finished the scarf, I gave it to our nurse for Christmas. She wears it all the time so I guess she really likes it.

Fringe

Add fringe to scarves and belts. Sew fringe to a doll's head and it becomes hair. A bunch of fringe is a horse's tail. Decorate the edges of a purse with fringe. For an unusual effect make long fringe and knot beads among the strands.

Alexandra D., age 15

INSTRUCTIONS

1 Cut pieces of yarn twice the desired length of the fringe.

2 Fold each piece of yarn in half and thread both ends through a large tapestry needle.

44

3 Pull the needle through the first cast-on stitch on the edge of a scarf, for example. Watch for the loop; don't pull it all the way through the stitch.

4 Draw the needle through the loop. Pull on both strands to tighten the loop.

5 On the cast-off side, fringe is put through the chain stitches. Elsewhere fringe can be put on as desired.

TWISTED CORD

Twisted cords can be made thick or thin, single or multicoloured and have as many different textures as there are kinds of yarn to twist. Use twisted cords for draw-strings in bags, ties on baby clothes, belts, hair ribbons, etc. While learning how to twist yarn into cord, make yourself a few hair-ribbons.

Hair-ribbons made by Katie D., age 9

MATERIAL NEEDED

Large amount of double knitting yarn
1 door knob
1 pencil
1 pair of scissors

INSTRUCTIONS

1   Measure out a piece of yarn the length of a hair-ribbon (try it around your head) and then cut a length of yarn 6 times that length.

2   Straighten out the cut piece of yarn and fold it in half. Hook the fold on a door knob and pull back both ends; tie a knot.

3   Put a pencil between the strands and slide it up against the knot. Pull the yarn tight, away from the door knob.

4 Hold the yarn very close to the pencil with one hand. With the index finger of the other hand turn the pencil like a propeller. Stop when the yarn is twisted all the way to the door knob.

7 Without slackening the yarn, hold the pencil up high and let the scissors dangle freely. You may have to stand on a chair so the scissors don't touch the floor. Let the scissors spin around. Stop them as soon as they start turning in the opposite direction.

Drawings by Caroline F., age 9

5 Now lay a pair of scissors across the twisted yarn. Have someone hold the scissors while you fold the yarn over them and bring the end with the pencil to the door knob. *Keep the yarn stretched tight at all times.*

6 Take the yarn off the door knob and loop it around the pencil, keeping the twisted yarn taut.

8 Slip the yarn off the pencil and *quickly*, before the cord has a chance to untwist, tie a knot 2·5 cm from the end. Remove the scissors and tie a knot at that end. Cut the yarn on the outside of each knot to form 2 little tassels.

Note: If you want to make a thicker cord use 2 or more strands of yarn. The finished cord looks pretty if the strands are different colours. If you use very thick rug yarn measure out 8 to 10 times the length of the finished twisted cord.

POMPONS

Pompons are fun to make. In various sizes and colours, they look adorable hanging in a bunch from the top of a baby's crib. Sew them to the ends of a tie string, on top of a ski hat, to ice-skate laces. Attach a tiny one to a zipper pull, key chain, or electric-light pull.

Pompon made by Tina A., age 14

MATERIAL NEEDED

Large amount of any yarn
1 cup or glass
1 small cotton reel
1 pair of scissors
Thin cardboard
1 large tapestry needle
1 pencil

INSTRUCTIONS

1 Holding a cup upside down near the edge of a piece of thin cardboard, make 2 circles by tracing around the cup.

2 Cut out the circles with scissors.

3 Place a small cotton reel in the centre of each circle and trace around it.

4 Cut out the inside circles, making 2 rings. Place 1 ring on top of the other.

5 Cut a piece of yarn 10 arms' length long. Fold it in half and wind it evenly around the 2 rings together, covering the entire surface of the rings. See illustration. Continue winding, pulling the yarn up through the hole, over the ring, and up through the hole again, until the hole is almost filled, using a tapestry needle to get the yarn through the hole as it fills up. You may want to use various colours of yarn.

6 Now slip one blade of the scissors down through the yarn and between the 2 cardboard rings and cut the yarn around the outer edge.

7 Cut 1 arm's length of yarn. Wind it tightly a few times around the middle between the 2 rings and tie a knot. Thread the yarn ends into the tapestry needle and draw them through the centre to the other side. Tie the ends together for hanging the ball, for sewing it to a hat, tie string, etc.

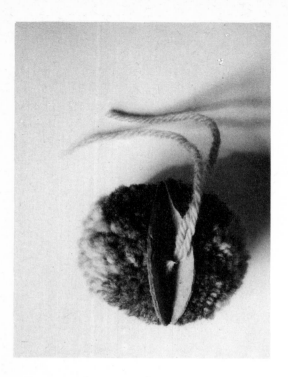

CHICKADEE

You can't imagine how lovable these birds are until you have felt how soft and fluffy they are. You might want to make a whole flock.

Buttercup is the name of my chick. She's all different shades of yellow but she has an orange beak and tiny green eyes. I cuddle with her at nighttime because she's so fluffy and soft. She likes to get under my covers and keep warm. It may sound silly that she's cold at night with all of that fur but she's only a chick.

Britt B., age 9

chickadee

8 Pull out the cardboard rings. Fluff up the ball by hitting it sharply against the edge of a table.

9 Trim the ball to a nicely rounded shape.

MATERIAL NEEDED

Large amount of any yarn
Cardboard for rings
1 small cotton reel
Felt for beak
Orange or white pipe cleaners for legs and feet
Black wool for eyes
1 tapestry needle

INSTRUCTIONS

1 Make 2 pompons, one teacup-size and one eggcup-size (see page 48); *but do not remove cardboard rings.*

2 Spread apart the 2 cardboard rings of each pompon and sew the pompons together closely at their centres.

3 Pull out the cardboard rings. Fluff up the pompons and trim them to the shape of a chick.

4 Cut a beak out of felt. Fold it in half and sew it with fine thread to the centre of the head.

5 Sew a piece of medium-thick black yarn through the head for eyes.

6 Fold a pipe cleaner in half and bend the ends to suggest feet. With fine thread sew the pipe cleaner to the bottom of the body.

MOTHER CAT AND KITTEN

These soft, cuddly cats are loved by children of all ages. Knit a whole family with each kitty a different colour, or knit tigers instead, with brown and yellow stripes. Here you will do the purl stitch for the first time.

MATERIAL NEEDED

1 small ball of double knitting yarn or some leftover yarn of same thickness in several colours.

1 pair of short knitting-needles, size 9 (See page 8.)

Stuffing material (See page 54.)

1 tapestry needle

1 small piece of ribbon

WORK METHOD

Casting on
Row knitting
Edge stitch
Joining yarn to change colours if knitting tigers
Casting off

PATTERN STITCH

Garter stitch
Purl stitch (See page 55.)

Knitted by Pamela E., Margot O., Julie B., Valerie D.

KNITTING INSTRUCTIONS

‡Edge stitch

Front and back are knitted as one piece, then folded at the top of the head.

Caroline F., age 9

Mother Cat

1 Cast on 16 stitches.

2 Knit all 16 stitches on the first row.

3‡ Knit until you have 13 garter-stitch rows. Finish knitting on an inside row.

4‡ Knit 1 row. ⎫
‡ Purl 1 row. ⎬ neck front
          ⎭

5‡ Knit 22 garter-stitch rows. Finish on an inside row.

6‡ Knit 1 row. ⎫
‡ Purl 1 row. ⎬ neck back
          ⎭

7‡ Knit 13 garter-stitch rows. Finish on an inside row.

8‡ Cast off. Leave 1 arm's length of yarn for sewing.

FINISHING INSTRUCTIONS

1 Fold the knitting in half and sew together as shown in illustration.

2 Stuff and then sew the bottom together.

3 Tie a ribbon around the neck.

4 Indicate ears with running stitches across the corners.

5 Embroider the face.

6 Make a tail:

   a Cut 3 pieces of yarn, each 1 arm's length.

   b Sew the three pieces to the back near the bottom.

   c Bring all the ends together and plait the three doubled strands. Tie a knot at the end.

Knitted by Valerie D., age 8

Materials for Stuffing

Many of the projects in this book call for stuffing material. To have stuffing when you need it, start collecting suitable material now in a special bag or box. Among the materials to collect are:

Cotton wool
Nylon stockings, cut into small pieces
Fabric, cut into small pieces
Bits and pieces of yarn
Unravelled yarn from old socks and pullovers

You can also stuff with hay and, of course, upholstery stuffing, which you can buy.

Note: Avoid shredded foam rubber, which is hard and bumpy.

Kitten

1 Cast on 8 stitches.

2‡ Knit all 8 stitches on the first row.

3‡ Knit until you have 7 garter-stitch rows. Finish on an inside row.

4‡ Knit 1 row. } neck front
  ‡ Purl 1 row. }

5‡ Knit 10 garter-stitch rows. Finish on an inside row.

6‡ Knit 1 row. } neck back
  ‡ Purl 1 row. }

7‡ Knit 7 garter-stitch rows. Finish on an inside row.

8‡ Cast off. Leave 1 arm's length of yarn for sewing.

Alexandra D., age 15

How to Do the Purl Stitch

(It's like making a knit stitch backwards.)

1 Bring the yarn in front of the left-hand needle, beside the stitch.

2 Put the tip of the right-hand needle under the yarn and through the stitch from back to front.

3 Pass the needle over the strand coming from the right index finger. Bring the needle around the yarn. Hold the yarn with your left thumb so it won't slide off the needle.

4 Bring the needle with the yarn on it back through the stitch.

5 Slide off the stitch on the left-hand needle and tighten the stitch on the right-hand needle.

6 Repeat steps 1 to 5 to the end of the row.

Stocking Stitch

The stocking-stitch pattern is the smoothest, most even knitting pattern. The outside shows nothing but knit stitches, while the inside is all purl stitches. It is frequently used for pullovers and mittens and is what you almost always see on the feet of stockings. The knit stitches in stocking stitch are easy to follow when embroidering or mending worn places.

Knitted by Diana H., age 14

KNITTING INSTRUCTIONS

Row Knitting. Knit all outside rows and purl all inside rows.
Round Knitting. Knit continuously for the same result.
You can count rows and rounds on either side, but it is easier to count them on the inside.

TEDDY BEAR

This teddy bear is about 17·5 cm tall. To make one twice as tall, double the number of stitches and rows in the instructions. By using thicker or thinner yarn and needles, you can also change the size.

Janine A., age 12

MATERIAL NEEDED

Three 25-gram balls of double knitting yarn
1 pair of short knitting-needles, size 9 (See page 8.)
Stuffing material (See page 54.)
1 tapestry needle

WORK METHOD

Casting on
Row knitting
Edge stitch
Casting off

PATTERN STITCH

Garter stitch
Purl stitch

Big bear knitted by Electra R., age 10

Small bears knitted by Serena R. and Alexandra S., age 12

The teddy bear is knitted in 5 parts.

57

KNITTING INSTRUCTIONS

‡Edge stitch

Arm (make 2)

1 Cast on 12 stitches.
2‡ Knit until you have 12 garter-stitch rows.
3‡ Cast off. Leave 1 arm's length of yarn for sewing.

Body and Head

1 Cast on 12 stitches.

2‡ Knit until you have 12 garter-stitch rows.

3‡ Knit 1 row. }
 ‡ Purl 1 row. } neck front

4‡ Knit 20 garter-stitch rows.

5‡ Knit 1 row. }
 ‡ Purl 1 row. } neck back

6‡ Knit 12 garter-stitch rows.

7‡ Cast off. Leave 1 arm's length of yarn for sewing.

Leg (make 2)

1 Cast on 12 stitches.

2‡ Knit until you have 12 garter-stitch rows.

3‡ Cast off. Leave 1 arm's length of yarn for sewing.

FINISHING INSTRUCTIONS

1 Fold and sew together 2 sides on each piece.

2 Stuff each part and sew the opening together.

3 Sew the arms and legs to the body.

4 Indicate ears with running-stitches across the corners as shown.

5 Embroider the face.

Caroline F., age 8,

PROJECT 12

HORSE

The size of this horse depends partly on the thickness of the yarn and needles. The small one was knitted on size 12 needles with very fine yarn and half the number of stitches and rows given in the instructions below.

WORK METHOD

Casting on
Row knitting
Edge stitch
Casting *in* stitches (See page 63.)
Casting off

PATTERN STITCH

Garter stitch

MATERIAL NEEDED

Any kind of yarn
1 pair of short knitting-needles
size depending on the thickness of yarn
(See page 7.)
Stuffing material (See page 54.)
1 tapestry needle
Felt or leather scraps for ears

Knitted by Margot O., age 12

KNITTING INSTRUCTIONS

‡Edge stitch

The horse is knitted as one piece. The same 2 needles are used throughout this project.

First Leg

1 Cast on 6 stitches.

2‡ Knit until you have 32 garter-stitch rows.

3‡ Do not cast off; but cut the yarn leaving about 10 cm.

Second Leg

1 Cast on 6 stitches onto the empty needle.

2‡ Using both needles, knit the second leg until you have 32 garter-stitch rows. Do not cut the yarn. (Both legs should be on one needle.)

Body

1‡ Knit the 6 stitches over the first leg on the needle, cast *in* 8 stitches (see page 63), knit the 6 stitches over the second leg. (You should now have 20 stitches on the needle.)

2‡ Knit until you have 8 garter-stitch rows over the 20 stitches.

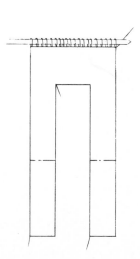

Neck

‡ Knit 8 garter-stitch rows over the first 6 stitches on the needle only, leaving the other stitches on the needle, but not knitting them.

Head

1 Cast *in* 6 stitches.

2‡ Knit 11 garter-stitch rows over the 12 stitches.

Neck

1‡ Cast off 6 stitches, then knit the 5 stitches remaining on the left-hand needle.

2‡ Knit 8 garter-stitch rows over the 6 stitches.

Body

1‡ Knit across the neck; then knit the 14 stitches that you are holding on the left-hand needle to finish the row.

2‡ Knit 8 garter-stitch rows over the 20 stitches.

3‡ Knit the first 6 stitches, then cast off 8 stitches and knit the 5 stitches

remaining on the left-hand needle for the third leg. (You have 12 stitches on the needle with a gap in between.)

Third Leg

1‡ Knit over the 6 stitches on the needle until you have 32 garter-stitch rows.

2‡ Cast off. Leave 1 arm's length of yarn for sewing.

Fourth Leg

1‡ With the yarn from the ball, knit over the 6 stitches on the needle as before, until you have 32 garter-stitch rows.

2‡ Cast off. Leave 1 arm's length of yarn for sewing.

FINISHING INSTRUCTIONS

1 Fold the legs in half and sew up the sides, stuffing as you go.

2 Fold the knitting in half with the open ends of the legs together. Sew the horse together, stuffing as you go.

3 Make a mane and a tail. (See page 44 for fringe.)

4 Embroider eyes and a mouth.

5 Sew on ears cut out of felt or leather.

How to Cast *in* Stitches

Casting *in* is a way to bring in new stitches after you have started to knit. It is usually done at the end of a row to extend the width.

KNITTING INSTRUCTIONS

1 Make a small loop, the yarn from the ball crossing in front.

2 Put the needle through the loop, front to back, and tighten the stitch. See drawing.

3 Repeat steps 1 and 2 for the required number of stitches.

DRAWSTRING BAG

You can knit a drawstring bag in cotton or wool and in various sizes to hold all kinds of things. Use bags to hold change, glasses, marbles, a compact, or school supplies. Make one of cotton twine and fill it with bits of soap for a soap glove to use in the shower. Fill another with pine needles or lavender blossoms and hang it in the linen cupboard.

Fannie I., age 8

Knitted by Serena R., age 11

KNITTING INSTRUCTIONS

Work out your own knitting instructions. Make your knitting twice the length that the bag will be, then fold it in half. Work edge stitch on each row. (For finishing, see page 140.) Make drawstrings of twisted cords (project 7) and weave them in and out between stitches with a small safety-pin. You might want to make a paper pattern to help in deciding on size, colour scheme, and pattern stitch for your bag. To know how many stitches to cast on you might want to make a knitting tension sample.

How to Check your Tension

A tension sample is a square of the pattern stitch, knitted with the yarn you plan to use, of 10 to 20 stitches. With it you can test *width* to know how many stitches to cast on and *length* for the number of rows to knit. If you find you are knitting 5 stitches to 2·5 cm, for example, you must cast on 25 stitches for a width of 12·5 cm.

Blocking

Blocking means to form the knitting into its final shape on a flat surface and to flatten down the stitches for an even, smooth appearance.

FOR BLOCKING BY HAND

1 Wash the knitting and pat it into shape on a towel on a flat surface.

2 Let dry.

FOR BLOCKING BY STEAM

Always block the pieces of a garment before sewing them together.

1 Turn knitting inside out and lay it on an ironing-board.

2 Pat into proper shape. Compare measurements with knitting instructions. Stretch lightly if necessary. Pin at corners and edges into the board to hold in shape.

3 Then either:

a Gently iron with a steam iron. Pat to smooth down stitches. Or:

b Cover knitting with a damp cloth (tea towel). Without pressing down, move a hot iron over the damp cloth to produce steam.

Laura B., age 11

Warning: Never steam garter-stitch rows or ribbing. To do so spoils the elastic quality. Do not press down on the iron. Never touch knitting directly with a hot iron.

DOLL'S BED

In this project you will again work out your own knitting instructions. The knitted pieces are small, so feel free to experiment, even at the risk of having to do something over again.

MATERIAL NEEDED

Small amounts of double knitting and 3 or 4 ply yarn
2 pairs of knitting-needles, sizes 11 and 9 (See page 7.)
A large kitchen matchbox or other box about 5 cm x 9 cm
1 handkerchief or piece of white cloth for pillow-case and sheets (optional)
Stuffing material (See page 54.)
1 tapestry needle

WORK METHOD

Casting on
Row knitting
Edge stitch
Joining yarn to change colours (optional)
Casting off

PATTERN STITCH

Garter stitch
Stocking stitch

KNITTING INSTRUCTIONS

You will be making the following:

1 mattress of double knitting yarn
1 blanket of double knitting yarn
1 pillow of 3 or 4 ply yarn
1 or 2 sheets of 3 or 4 ply yarn or use a small white handkerchief for a sheet.

1 Make 2 tension samples each 10 stitches wide to use for measuring. Make one of double knitting yarn with size 9 needles and another of 3 or 4 ply yarn with size 11 needles.

2 Use your samples to find out how many stitches to cast on for each piece of knitting. (See page 65.) Make the mattress the width of the bed, and the pillow a little narrower. You may or may not want the blanket and sheet to tuck in.

3 Mattress and pillow are knitted double length, then folded in half, sewn, and lightly stuffed.

4 Finish off each piece with care.

Much joy!

BABY DOLL

This doll is small enough to fit nicely into the little doll's bed. (See page 66.)

MATERIAL NEEDED

A small quantity of 3 or 4 ply yarn
1 pair of short knitting-needles, size 11
1 piece of nylon stocking (for head)
Stuffing material
Fur for the hair, or make it of yarn fringe
Glue
1 tapestry needle

WORK METHOD

Row knitting
Edge stitch
Casting off

PATTERN STITCH

Garter stitch
Stocking stitch

KNITTING INSTRUCTIONS

‡Edge stitch

Front

1 Cast on 26 stitches.

2‡ Knit 2 rows.

3 Slip the first stitch, knit 7 stitches, purl 10 stitches, knit 8 stitches.

4‡ Knit 1 row.

5 Repeat steps 3 and 4 once.

6 Again slip the first stitch, knit 7 stitches, purl 10 stitches, knit 8 stitches.

7‡ Cast off 8 stitches, then knit the 17 stitches remaining on the left-hand needle.

8‡ Cast off 8 stitches, knit the 9 stitches remaining on the left-hand needle.

9‡ Knit 12 garter-stitch rows.

10‡ Cast off. Leave 1 arm's length of yarn for sewing.

Back

1 Cast on 26 stitches.

2‡ Knit until you have 4 garter-stitch rows.

3‡ Cast off 8 stitches, knit the 17 stitches remaining on the left-hand needle.

4‡ Cast off 8 stitches, then knit the 9 stitches remaining on the left-hand needle.

5‡ Knit until you have 17 garter-stitch rows, counting from the cast-on edge.

6‡ Cast off. Leave 1 arm's length of yarn for sewing.

FINISHING INSTRUCTIONS

1 Sew the front and back together. Leave open at the top.

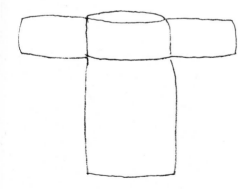

2 Stuff the arms lightly.

3 For the head, form a ball of stuffing and stretch the piece of nylon stocking around it. Tie it together securely with a piece of yarn. See illustration.

4 Place the head between the shoulders and sew the edges together, so that the head is held in place.

5 Sew in all yarn ends.

6 For hair, glue a bit of fur to the head, or use yarn fringe.

7 Embroider a face if you wish, or leave it to your imagination.

69

BABY BOOTEES: 1 TO 3 MONTHS

Make these bootees and give them to a mother for her baby. Instead of casting off to finish this knitting, you will end by knitting together stitches at the toe of the bootee.

Make 2 bootees. Right and left are the same. The bootee is folded in half at the bottom of the foot.

MATERIAL NEEDED

Three 25-gram balls of 3 ply yarn
1 pair of short knitting-needles, size 11
(See page 8.)
1 metre of silk ribbon or handmade cord
(See page 46 for twisted cord.)
1 tapestry needle
1 small safety-pin

WORK METHOD

Casting on
Row knitting
Edge stitch
Casting off
Ending off by decreasing (See page 72.)

PATTERN STITCH

Garter stitch

Knitted by Wendy B., age 13

70

KNITTING INSTRUCTIONS

‡Edge stitch

1 Cast on 58 stitches.

2‡ Knit until you have 15 garter-stitch rows or 5·7 cm. Finish on an inside row.

3‡ Cast off 12 stitches. Knit the 45 stitches remaining on the left-hand needle.

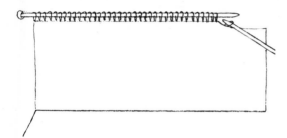

4‡ Cast off 12 stitches. Knit the 33 stitches remaining on the left-hand needle. (You should have 34 stitches on the row.)

5‡ Knit 9 garter-stitch rows (24 counting from the cast-on edge, or 9 cm).

6 Ending off by decreasing

   a‡ Knit together 2 stitches. Repeat to end of row. (You should have 18 stitches left on the row.)

   b‡ Knit 1 row.

   c‡ Knit together 2 stitches. Repeat to end of row. (You should have 10 stitches left on the needle.)

   d‡ Knit 1 row.

7 Cut the yarn leaving 1 arm's length for sewing. Using a tapestry needle draw the yarn through the 10 stitches on the needle. See illustration. Remove the knitting needle. Draw the yarn through again in the same direction and pull the stitches together tightly.

FINISHING INSTRUCTIONS

1 Fold the knitting in half and sew the bootee together.

2 Attach the ribbon or cord to a safety pin. Weave it over and under 2 garter-stitch rows all around the bootee. See photograph. Cut the ends diagonally to keep the fabric from fraying.

Knitted by Janine A., age 12, using double knitting yarn and the same number of stitches

Ending Off by Decreasing

You usually end off row knitting by casting off. Another way is to decrease the number of stitches rapidly until there are only a few left. Those last few stitches are then strung onto the yarn end and gathered together tightly. This makes a slightly rounded ending.

KNITTING INSTRUCTIONS

1 Knit or purl together 2 stitches. Repeat to end of row.

2 Work 1 row in your pattern stitch.

3 Repeat steps 1 and 2.

4 Cut the yarn and string the stitches remaining onto it.

Katri B. with her little brother

SLIPPERS

These warm, comfortable slippers make good presents because they stretch to fit almost any foot. You may also want to make a cotton bag to carry them in when travelling.

Jennifer M., age 10

MATERIAL NEEDED

Ten 25-gram balls of double knitting yarn
1 pair of short knitting-needles, size 6
1 large tapestry needle

WORK METHOD

Row knitting
Edge stitch
Ending off by decreasing

PATTERN STITCH

Garter stitch
Ribbing (See page 75).

KNITTING INSTRUCTIONS

‡Edge stitch

Knit with double yarn, using the yarn from 2 balls at the same time. This reinforces the slipper for greater strength and longer wear.

1 Cast on 32 stitches.

2 Knit tightly. Knit 10 stitches, then purl 1, knit 10, purl 1, knit 10.

3‡ Knit 1 row.

4 Slip the first stitch directly to the right-hand needle, then knit 9, purl 1, knit 10, purl 1, knit 10.

5‡ Knit 1 row.

6‡ Follow step 4 for all inside rows and knit all outside rows until you have knitted 15 garter-stitch rows.

7‡ Rib 18 rows: purl 1, knit 1.

8 Ending off by decreasing:

　a‡ Knit together 2 stitches. Repeat to end of row. (You should now have 17 stitches left on the needle.)

　b‡ Purl 1 row.

9 Cut the yarn, leaving 1 arm's length. Using a large tapestry needle, draw the yarn through the stitches. Remove the knitting needle. Draw the yarn through again in the same direction and pull the stitches together tightly.

74

FINISHING INSTRUCTIONS

1 Fold the knitting in half.

2 Sew together the knitting at the heel and for the length of the ribbing at the toe.

3 Sew in all yarn ends.

Caroline F., age 9, making a twisted cord (see page 46)

The Ribbing Pattern

In the ribbing pattern, ribs or ridges run up and down the knitting at right angles to the needle. Because the pattern is elastic, it is used for borders on sweaters, socks, hats and mittens. As the pattern for an entire garment, ribbing has an interesting texture and fits snugly. The ridges are formed of knit stitches. The valleys are purl stitches.

KNITTING INSTRUCTIONS

The most common ribbing patterns are the following: knit 1 stitch, purl 1 stitch; knit 2, purl 2. See illustrations.

The first row is knitted according to the chosen pattern. In all following rows knit stitches are worked above knit stitches and purl stitches are worked above purl stitches, to form knit ribs and purl valleys.

Hold the yarn at the back to knit, bring it forward to purl.

For a tighter fitting border cast the stitches onto one of the regular needles, then knit them off and rib the border on needles a few sizes thinner. After finishing the border change back to the regular needles.

Knitted by Catherine S., age 12

Knitted for her brother by Laura B., age 10

SKI HAT

There is a variety of designs to choose from if you want to embroider your ski hat (see page 78). Or you might want to make your own pattern on graph paper. You could also design your own hat and then work out the knitting instructions. Measure tightly around your head with a strip of paper and cast on stitches to fit this measurement. End off your own creation the same way as the ski hat below (steps 6 and 7).

MATERIAL NEEDED

Six 25-gram balls of double knitting yarn
1 pair of short knitting-needles, size 9
(See page 8.)
Contrasting colours of the same kind of yarn for embroidering
1 tapestry needle

WORK METHOD

Casting on
Row knitting
Edge stitch
Ending off by decreasing

PATTERN STITCH

Ribbing
Stocking stitch

KNITTING INSTRUCTIONS

‡Edge stitch

You may want to work the ribbing on smaller needles for a tighter fit. (See page 75.)

1 Cast on 118 stitches.

2‡ Rib 3 rows: knit 2, purl 2.

3‡ Work 20 rows or about 5·7 cm of stocking stitch by knitting on the outside and purling on the inside

4‡ Rib 23 rows or about 6 cm. *Finish ribbing on an outside row.*

5‡ Work 12·5 cm of stocking stitch *but this time* knit on the *inside* and purl on the *outside*.

6 End off by decreasing:

   a‡ Knit together 2 stitches. Repeat to end of row. (You should have 60 stitches on the needle.)

   b‡ Purl 1 row.

   c‡ Knit together 2 stitches. Repeat to end of row. (You should now have 31 stitches.)

   d‡ Purl 1 row.

7 Cut the yarn, leaving 1 arm's length. Using a tapestry needle, draw the yarn through the stitches. Remove the knitting needle. Draw the yarn through again in the same direction and pull stitches together tightly.

FINISHING INSTRUCTIONS

1 Block the stocking-stitch part of the knitting; *be careful not to steam the ribbing*.

2 Sew the hat together and sew in all yarn ends.

3 Embroider design. (See page 144 for Swiss darning stitch.)

KNITTING SQUARES

A knitted square has four sides, which must be equal. There are three ways to knit squares. You can make them any size you want.

You can knit squares out of pieces of leftover yarn. Fine yarn can be used double to match the thickness of heavier yarn. Then the squares can be sewn together to make a poncho, a scarf, a hat. Two squares can be sewn together to make a bag. Knitting a patchwork blanket of squares can become a family project.

Either knit the squares in whatever colours you have and then arrange them in a pattern, or make a colour sketch first and carefully follow it.

MATERIAL NEEDED

Odds and ends of yarn
Knitting-needles (See page 7.)

WORK METHOD

Casting on
Row knitting
Edge stitch
Increasing stitches with yarn-overs (See page 82.)
Increasing by knitting 2 stitches out of 1 stitch (See page 82.)

Knitted by Swiss children, aged 11–12

79

Decreasing by knitting together stitches
(See page 83.)
Casting off

PATTERN STITCH

For straight method – any pattern stitch
For right-angle method – garter stitch
For diagonal method – garter stitch

KNITTING INSTRUCTIONS

‡Edge stitch
Select one of the following three methods.

Right-Angle Method

1   Cast on 5 stitches.

2   Knit all stitches on the first row.

3   For the next row slip the first stitch, yarn-over, knit the 3 middle stitches, yarn-over, knit the last stitch.

4‡ Knit one row. You should now have 7 stitches on the needle because of the yarn-overs.

5‡ Knit to the 3 middle stitches, yarn-over before and after the middle stitches, then knit to the end of the row.

6‡ Knit one row. There are now 9 stitches.

7‡ Continue as above, alternating between steps 5 and 6, increasing every other row.

8‡ Cast off.

Note: To check the size of the square, knit to the centre of any row. Place the knitting flat on a table and position the needles at right angles.

80

Diagonal Method

1 Cast on 3 stitches.

2 Knit all stitches on the first row.

3 On the next row, slip the first stitch, knit to the last stitch, then increase by knitting 2 stitches out of the last stitch. (See page 82.)

4 Repeat step 3 until the knitting has reached the right width.

5‡ From now on decrease by knitting together the last 2 stitches on every row until you have only 3 stitches left on the needle.

6‡ Cast off.

Straight Method

1 Cast on as many stitches as you need to make the square the size you want.

2‡ Knit the same number of garter-stitch rows as you have stitches on the needle, or until the piece is exactly square. Fold diagonally to test length.

3‡ Cast off.

Design for poncho by Amy M., age 15

How to Make a Yarn Over

Knitting

Knit to the place where you want the yarn-over to be. Then bring the yarn to the front and over the right-hand needle, making a loop over the needle. Hold the yarn on the needle and continue to knit.

Purling

Purl to the place where you want the yarn-over to be. Then again bring the yarn to the front and over the needle and back to the front ready to purl the next stitch.

Different Ways to Increase Stitches

You can increase the width of your knitting these three ways:

1 *Knitting 2 stitches out of 1*
At the place where you want to add a stitch make a knit stitch, but leave the old stitch on the left-hand needle. Knit through it again but at the back of the needle.

2 *Making a stitch from a yarn-over*
Where you want to add a stitch make a yarn-over. In the following row knit the yarn-over just as you would any other stitch. To avoid leaving a hole you can knit through the back of the yarn-over, which gives it a twist.

82

3 *Adding stitches by casting in*

a Make a small loop, the yarn from the ball crossing in front.

b Put the needle through the loop, front to back, and tighten the stitch.

Shivan S., age 8

Different Ways to Decrease Stitches

There are three ways to decrease 1 stitch:

1 *Knit decreasing*—knit together 2 stitches.

2 *Purl decreasing*—purl together 2 stitches.

3 *Slip decreasing*—slip 1 stitch, knit 1 stitch, then pass the slipped stitch over the knitted stitch.

There are three ways to decrease 2 stitches:

1 *Double knit decreasing*—knit together 3 stitches.

2 *Double purl decreasing*—purl together 3 stitches.

3 *Double slip decreasing*—slip 1 stitch, knit together 2 stitches, then pass the slipped stitch over the knitted stitch.

83

BABY BIB

This pretty little bib for an infant is made of cotton yarn and is machine-washable. You may want to crochet a border.

MATERIAL NEEDED

1 ball of 4 ply cotton yarn
1 pair of short knitting-needles, size 11
(See page 8.)
1 tapestry needle

WORK METHOD

Casting on
Row knitting
Edge stitch
Increasing by knitting 2 stitches out of 1
Decreasing by knitting together stitches

PATTERN STITCH

Garter stitch

KNITTING INSTRUCTIONS

‡Edge stitch

1   Cast on 3 stitches (bottom corner).

2   Knit all stitches on the first row.

3   Slip the first stitch, knit to the last stitch, then increase by knitting 2 stitches out of the last stitch. (See page 82.)

4   Repeat step 3 until the knitting is from 16·5 to 18 cm wide. Finish with an even number.

5‡ Knit to the centre of the row. Turn the knitting around. (Hold the other half of the stitches on the needle, but do not knit them. From now on you will be knitting each half separately.)

6‡ Decrease by knitting together the last 2 stitches on every row until there are only 3 stitches left on the needle.

7‡ Cast off.

8‡ Knit the second half the same as the first, by starting at the centre and following steps 5 and 6.

FINISHING INSTRUCTIONS

1 Sew in all yarn ends.

2 For the tie strings

  a Make a slipknot and place it loosely onto a knitting needle.

  b Poke the needle through one of the top corners, wrap the yarn once around the needle, and bring the needle with the yarn on it back through the same place in the corner.

c Wrap the yarn once more around the needle and draw it through the 2 stitches on the needle.

  d Finger crochet a tie string about 28 cm long.

  e Repeat for other corner.

Florian H., 4 months

DESIGNING PATTERNS WITH KNIT AND PURL STITCHES

Design your own knitting patterns using these symbols:

| for a knit stitch

—   for a purl stitch

Draw your design on graph paper, using the 2 symbols to represent the stitches as they will appear on the outside of the knitting project. Draw enough of the pattern to visualize what it will look like.

HOW TO USE YOUR KNITTING DIAGRAM

This knitting diagram represents the pattern of the knitting in the photograph. The knitting diagrams in this book only tell you what the knitting will *look* like on the outside. It is up to you to work out what stitches to knit to get the patterns indicated on the diagrams.

In row knitting be especially careful that your stitches come out the same as on the diagram. (A purl stitch on the inside is a knit stitch on the outside.)

FITTING THE DIAGRAM TO YOUR KNITTING

Count the stitches in one sequence of a row (circled parts of diagrams). The number of stitches you will cast on must be a multiple of the number in one sequence. If necessary, add or subtract a few stitches to make the pattern fit or to make it look the same at both edges. For row knitting, add 2 stitches for the edge stitch.

88

90

KNITTING LACE PATTERNS

To read the diagrams in this book for lace patterns or to design your own lace patterns, you will need to know the following knitting symbols:

1 | for a knit stitch.

2   —   for a purl stitch.

3   ⟋| for 2 knit stitches knitted together.

4   =   for 2 purl stitches knitted together.

5   ⟍   for a slip decrease stitch. (Slip 1 stitch, knit the second stitch, then pass the slipped stitch over the knitted stitch.)

6   ∩   for a yarn-over.

7   ⌒⌒   for 2 yarn-overs.

(Place the yarn over the right-hand needle from front to back twice. In the following row, knit the first yarn-over and purl the second.)

8   ≡   for 3 purl stitches knitted together.

9   ⋀   for a double slip decrease stitch. (Slip the first stitch, knit together 2 stitches, then pass the slipped stitch over the knitted decreasing stitch.)

Note: In the diagrams for lace patterns yarn-overs are always balanced by decreasing to keep the number of stitches on the needle the same.

Beth P., age 12

PROJECT 21

BABY BONNET

This bonnet is for infants 1 day to 3 months old. Among the patterns suggested here, the lace patterns would be best for spring while the solid patterns would be warmer for winter.

MATERIAL NEEDED

Three 25-gram balls of 4 ply yarn
1 pair of knitting-needles, size 11 (See page 8.)
1 metre of narrow ribbon or a hand-made, twisted tie string. (See page 46.)

WORK METHOD

Casting on
Row knitting
Edge stitch
Star end-decreasing (see photograph)

PATTERN STITCH

Choose from among photographs. Then use the corresponding diagram to figure out how to knit that pattern. (See page 91 for key to symbols.)

Amy M., age 15

KNITTING INSTRUCTIONS

‡Edge stitch

1 Cast on number given under photograph.

2‡ Rib 1·3 cm, knit 1, purl 1.

3‡ Work 9 cm in the pattern stitch. Finish knitting on an inside row.

Cast on 84 stitches

Cast on 83 stitches

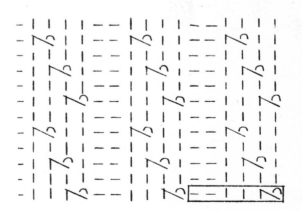

Cast on 84 stitches

95

4 To shape top:
Star end-decrease:

a‡ Purl together 2 stitches, knit 8, repeat to end of row. Knit any leftover stitches.

b‡ Purl 1 row.

c‡ Purl together 2 stitches, knit 7, repeat to end of row. Knit any leftover stitches.

d‡ Purl 1 row.

e‡ Purl together 2 stitches, knit 6, repeat to end of row. Knit any leftover stitches.

f ‡ Purl 1 row.

Continue to decrease as above, knitting 5, 4, 3, 2, 1, 0, and knitting any leftover stitches.

5 Cut the yarn, leaving 1 arm's length. Using a tapestry needle, draw the yarn through the stitches left on the needle. Remove the needle. Draw the yarn through the stitches again in the same direction and pull the stitches together tightly.

FINISHING INSTRUCTIONS

1 Block by steaming. If knitting needs to be washed, block by patting it into shape when wet on a flat surface and allow to dry.

2 Fold the bonnet in half and sew the rounded edge together.

3 Sew the tie strings to the corners. Cut the ends diagonally to prevent fraying.

Beatrice R., age 12. Sew a drawstring bag to carry your knitting.

PROJECT 22

BABY SWEATER: 1 TO 8 MONTHS

This little sweater is knitted all in one piece. You knit from side to side instead of the usual bottom to top. It can be worn with the opening at the front or the back.

MATERIAL NEEDED

Four 25-gram balls of fine baby yarn

1 pair of knitting-needles, size 11 (See page 8.)
1 stitch holder 10 cm long
1 metre of narrow ribbon or a hand-made, twisted tie string (See page 46.)
1 tapestry needle

WORK METHOD

Casting on
Row knitting
Edge stitch
Casting *in* stitches
Casting off
Eyelet holes (See page 102.)

Knitted by Ritchie P., age 13

97

PATTERN STITCH

Choose from among photographs. Then use the corresponding diagram to work out how to knit that pattern. (See page 91 for key to symbols.)

KNITTING INSTRUCTIONS

‡Edge stitch

First Half of Front

1 Cast on 70 stitches.

2‡ Knit until you have 4 garter-stitch rows (border).

3‡ (Outside row) Work 52 stitches in your pattern stitch or until there are 17 stitches on the needle. These will be knitted in garter-stitch rows to form the yoke. See photograph.

4 Yoke: knit together 2 stitches. Turn the knitting around to the inside row and yarn-over once on the inside with the right-hand needle. Knit 1 stitch. See drawing. Finish the row (53 stitches) in your pattern stitch.

Note: By turning the knitting around you skipped knitting the 17 stitches for the yoke.

5‡ (Outside row) Work in your pattern stitch to 1 stitch before the yarn-over you made in the last row.

6 Yoke: knit 1 stitch. Knit the yarn-over but keep it on the left-hand needle. See illustration 1. Knit together the same yarn-over and the next stitch. See illustration 2. Knit to end of row.

7‡ (Inside row) Knit the 17 yoke stitches. Finish the row in your pattern stitch.

8‡ (Outside row) Work in your pattern stitch until there are 17 stitches left for the yoke. Knit the yoke stitches.

9‡ (Inside row) Knit the 17 yoke stitches. Finish the row in your pattern stitch.

Note: You should now have a small hole at the beginning of the yoke and 2 garter-stitch rows knitted beyond it. Compare your knitting with the photograph. At this point it is necessary to turn the knitting. The small hole and others to come will be used as markers.

10 Repeat steps 3 to 9 until the knitting measures 14 cm. Finish knitting on an inside row.

First Sleeve

1‡ (Outside row) Work 41 stitches and put them on a stitch holder. Continue knitting the row.

2 Work the stitches on the inside row. Cast *in* 41 stitches. Make sure you again have 70 stitches on the needle.

3‡ Work about 15 cm for the sleeve.

Finish knitting on an inside row.

100

Compare the pattern stitch on the sleeve with that on the front where you are holding the stitches. The front must have 1 extra row.

4‡ (Outside row) Cast off 41 stitches. Continue knitting the row.

5‡ (Inside row) Work the stitches on the needle. Put the stitches that are on the stitch holder onto the empty needle. See illustration. Finish row.

Back

‡Work 20 cm for the back. Finish knitting on an inside row.

Second Sleeve

Work the same as the first sleeve.

Second Half of Front

1‡ Work 12·5 cm ending with a border of garter-stitch rows.

2‡ Cast off. Do not cut the yarn. Leave the last stitch on the needle.

Completing Yoke

1 Pick up and knit one stitch between each 2 garter-stitch rows along the edge on the outside of the yoke. See photograph. Do this by inserting the tip of the needle, front to back, between the first 2 garter-stitch rows. Then wrap the yarn around the tip and bring the yarn through to the front.

2‡ Knit 1 row.

3‡ Work 1 row of eyelet holes: knit together 2 stitches, yarn-over. Repeat to end of row.

4‡ Knit 1 row.

5‡ Cast off. Cut the yarn leaving 7·5 cm

Completing Sleeves

1 Make a slipknot and put it on the needle. Pick up and knit 36–40 (even number) stitches along the edge of the sleeve.

2‡ Rib 6·5 cm: knit 1, purl 1.

3‡ Cast off in the ribbing pattern. Leave 1 arm's length of yarn for sewing the sleeve together.

FINISHING INSTRUCTIONS

1 Block. (See page 65.)

2 Sew the sleeves together on the inside with overcasting stitches.

3 Sew in all yarn ends.

4 Weave in ribbon. Cut ribbon diagonally to keep the fabric from fraying.

Picking up Stitches

By 'picking up stitches' along an edge you can add new knitting to finished work. The picked-up stitches are put onto a needle and knitted as usual. The process is often used to add borders around the neck, waist, wrist or ankle. You can also pick up stitches to lengthen the sleeves and waist of a sweater you have outgrown.

KNITTING INSTRUCTIONS

Insert the tip of the needle, front to back, through the top edge of the knitting. Then wrap the yarn around the tip and bring the yarn through to the front (similar to crocheting).

Eyelet Holes

Making a row of eyelet holes is usually done so you can thread a tie string through the holes.

IN GARTER STITCH AND STOCKING STITCH

1 Yarn-over, knit together 2 stitches. Repeat to end of row or round.

2 Next row or round: knit each yarn-over into a regular stitch.

WITHIN THE RIBBING PATTERN: KNIT 1, PURL 1

1 Yarn-over before the purl stitch, then knit together the knit and purl stitches. Repeat to end of row or round.

2 a Row knitting: next row work all yarn-overs as knit stitches, purling in between.

b Round knitting: in the next round work all yarn-overs as purl stitches, knitting the stitches in between.

WITHIN THE RIBBING PATTERN: KNIT 2, PURL 2

1 Slip the second knit stitch, purl 1, then bring the second slip stitch over the purl stitch, yarn-over twice. Knit together the second purl stitch and the first knit stitch. Repeat to end of row or round.

2 Next row or round: purl the first yarn-over and knit the second one, otherwise follow your ribbing pattern.

MITTENS FOR AN INFANT

These mittens will nicely fit an infant up to 3 months. They do not need thumbs because babies keep their hands in a fist.

Alexandra D., age 15

MATERIAL NEEDED

Three 25-gram balls of 3 or 4 ply yarn
1 set of 4 short double-pointed knitting-needles, size 11 (See page 8.)
1 metre of narrow ribbon or a hand-made, twisted tie string (See page 46.)
1 tapestry needle

WORK METHOD

Casting on stitches for round knitting (See page 106.)
Round knitting
Eyelet holes
Ending off with 3 stitches between decreasing (See page 106.)

PATTERN STITCH

Ribbing
Stocking stitch

103

KNITTING INSTRUCTIONS

These are for 1 mitten. Make 2.

1 Cast on 40 stitches, 14 on each of 2 needles and 12 on a third needle.

2 Rib 4 cm: knit 1, purl 1.

3 Work 1 round of eyelet holes: yarn-over, slip the knit stitch, purl 1, then pull the slip stitch over the purl stitch and let it go. Repeat to end of round.

4 Knit 1 round. You should still have 14 stitches on each of the first 2 needles and 12 on the third.

5 Knit 5 cm.

6 End off with 3 stitches between decreasing:

Note: Instead of purl decreasing as instructed, you can slip decrease, which blends better into the stocking-stitch background. See illustration on page 83.

104

a Rearrange the stitches on the needles to 15/10/15.

b Purl together 2 stitches, knit 3, repeat to end of round.

c Knit 3 rounds.

d Purl together 2 stitches, knit 2, repeat to end of round.

e Knit 2 rounds.
   repeat to end of round..

f Purl together 2 stitches, knit 1,

g Knit 1 round.

h Purl together 2 stitches, repeat to end of round.

7 Cut the yarn, leaving about 20 cm. Using a tapestry needle, draw the yarn through the stitches. Remove the knitting-needles. Draw the yarn through the stitches again in the same direction and pull them together tightly.

FINISHING INSTRUCTIONS

1 Bring the yarn to the inside of the knitting and sew it in.

2 Pull the casting-on yarn through the tiny knot, then sew it in on the inside.

3 Weave the tie string through the eyelet holes. Cut the ends of narrow ribbon diagonally to prevent fraying.

Round Knitting

For round knitting (knitting in circles instead of back and forth in rows), you use a set of 4 or 5 double-pointed needles. You cast on stitches onto all the needles except the one you will knit with. If the knitting is unusually wide you should cast onto more than 4 needles in order not to have more than 20 stitches on a needle.

In round knitting you are always knitting on the outside. *Each round starts at the piece of yarn left over from casting on (see illustration on page 106). The round is completed when you have knitted around to that same point.* You just keep knitting around and around, and the knitting grows longer.

Because there are no "sides" to round knitting, there is no edge stitch to think about. All stitches are knitted.

Casting On Stitches onto 3 Needles

1 Measure out enough yarn for casting on.

2 Cast on 1/3 of the stitches onto the first needle. Slide the stitches to the middle of the needle and let it dangle.

3 Cast on the second 1/3 of the stitches onto the second needle. Make sure there is no gap between stitches from one needle to the next. See illustration. Slide the stitches to the middle of the needle and let it dangle.

4 Cast on the rest of the stitches onto the third needle. Slide them to the middle of the needle.

5 Form a triangle with the needles. See illustration. Slide the stitches on the first needle towards the point and knit them off onto the empty needle.

Ending Off in Round Knitting

To make a rounded ending like that on a sock, mitten or hat, you decrease *1 stitch* at a time at regular intervals for an entire round. (Choose decreasing method from page 83.) Decreasing rounds are alternated with a certain number of regular rounds until the knitting comes to an end.

When you are ready to end off the knitting, you must know how many regular stitches to knit between decreasing stitches. Most of the time the instructions will tell you. But if you designed your own project, you would have to work it out this way: Divide the stitches on the round by 10 and subtract 1. (If 10 doesn't fit exactly, use the nearest number that 10 does divide into.)

EXAMPLE

Stitches on round	Formula	Stitches between decreasing
72	$70 \div 10 - 1 =$	6
36	$40 \div 10 - 1 =$	3

Start the decreasing round by purling together 2 stitches. Knit the number of in-between stitches you worked out by the above formula. Alternate decreasing and knit stitches to end of round. Then knit the same number of regular rounds as the number of stitches between decreasing stitches. In each succeeding decreasing round the number of stitches between decreasing stitches is reduced by 1, and so is the number of regular rounds knitted on top.

Note: Instead of purling together you can knit together 2 stitches or slip decrease (see page 83.)

If there are 6 stitches between decreasing, follow steps 1 to 8

1 Purl together 2 stitches, knit 6, repeat to end of round.
Knit any leftover stitches.
Knit 6 rounds.

If there are 5 stitches between decreasing, follow steps 2 to 8

2 Purl together 2 stitches, knit 5,
repeat to end of round. Knit 5 rounds.

If there are 4 stitches between decreasing, follow steps 3 to 8

3 Purl together 2 stitches, knit 4, repeat to end of round.
Knit 4 rounds.

If there are 3 stitches between decreasing, follow steps 4 to 8

4 Purl together 2 stitches, knit 3, repeat to end of round.
Knit 3 rounds.

If there are 2 stitches between decreasing, follow steps 5 to 8

5 Purl together 2 stitches, knit 2, repeat to end of round.
Knit 2 rounds.

If there is 1 stitch between decreasing, follow steps 6 to 8

6 Purl together 2 stitches, knit 1, repeat to end of round.
Knit 1 round.

If there are 0 stitches between decreasing, follow steps 7 and 8.

7 Purl together 2 stitches, repeat to end of round.

8 Cut the yarn at 1 arm's length. Thread it through a tapestry needle. String the remaining stitches onto the yarn and draw them together tightly.

Pamela M., age 13

SKI MITTENS

Mittens keep your hands warmer than gloves. They are also easier to knit. For skiing, sew suede, felt or leather to the palms and on the inside of the thumbs. The knitting instructions below are for a mitten to fit a 12-year-old. For a different size, trace around the hand. Then knit a tension sample and see how many stitches you need to fit across the palm. Double this and add 4 stitches for the thickness of the hand. This will give you the number of stitches to cast on.

MATERIAL NEEDED

Five 25-gram balls of double knitting yarn.
1 set of 4 short, double-pointed knitting-needles, size 9 (See page 8.)
1 tapestry needle

WORK METHOD

Casting on
Round knitting
Increasing stitches from yarn-overs
Ending off with 3 stitches between decreasing

PATTERN STITCH

Ribbing
Stocking stitch

Knitted by Margot O., age 12

108

109

KNITTING INSTRUCTIONS

These instructions are for 1 mitten; make 2 (left and right are the same). They fit the traced hand of a 12-year-old. (See page 109.)

1 Cast on 36 stitches, 12/12/12.

2 Rib about 7·5 cm for the cuff: knit 2, purl 2.

3 Knit 4 rounds.

4 Place a marker at the beginning of the round. At this point start to increase stitches for the thumb as follows:

   a Yarn-over onto the empty needle, knit the first 2 stitches on the round, yarn-over, then knit the rest of the round.

   b Knit 2 rounds. In the first of the 2 rounds knit through the back of each of the 2 yarn-overs. This twists the stitches and avoids a hole.

   c Yarn-over onto the empty needle, knit 4, yarn-over, then knit the rest of the round.

   d Knit 2 rounds.

   e Yarn-over onto the empty needle, knit 6, yarn-over, then knit the rest of the round.

   f Knit 2 rounds.

   g Yarn-over onto the empty needle, knit 8, yarn-over, then knit the rest of the round.

   h Knit 2 rounds.

   i Yarn-over onto the empty needle, knit 10, yarn-over, then knit the rest of the round.

   j Knit 2 rounds.

   k String the first 12 stitches of the round onto a piece of different coloured yarn and keep them aside for knitting the thumb later.

110

See illustration above. There should be 10 stitches left on the needle.

5 Cast *in* 2 stitches onto the empty needle. Knit 1 round. You should now have 12 stitches on each needle.

6 Knit about 8 cm or as many rounds as needed to cover the tip of the little finger.

7 Rearrange the stitches on the needle to 10/15/11. End off with 3 stitches between decreasing. (See page 106.)

COMPLETING THE THUMB

1 Transfer the stitches you are holding on the yarn onto 3 needles, 4/4/4.

2 With the third needle pick up 2 stitches to bridge the gap at the base of the thumb. See illustration. You should now have 14 stitches for knitting the thumb.

3 Knit as many rounds as needed to cover the thumb.

4 Rearrange the stitches to 3/6/5. End off the thumb with 1 stitch between decreasing.

5 Cut the yarn, leaving 10 cm. Using a tapestry needle draw the yarn through the stitches. Remove the knitting-needles. Draw the yarn through again in the same direction and pull the stitches together tightly.

FINISHING INSTRUCTIONS

1 Sew in yarn ends. (See page 140.)

2 Sew a few stitches over the gap at the base of the thumb if needed.

Knitted by Julia M., age 13

DOLLS

Fine-Yarn Doll

These dolls are about 30 cm tall. You can knit pullovers, socks, scarves and hats for them by following the instructions in this book. Knit a tension sample and fit it on the body of the doll for the number of stitches to cast on.

MATERIAL NEEDED

Three 25-gram balls of 2, 3 or 4 ply yarn
1 set of short double-pointed knitting-needles, size 11 (See page 8.)
Stuffing material (See page 54.)
1 tapestry needle

WORK METHOD

Casting on
Round knitting
Row knitting
Edge stitch
Casting *in* stitches
Ending off with 2 stitches between decreasing
Casting off

PATTERN STITCH

Ribbing
Stocking stitch

112

KNITTING INSTRUCTIONS

‡Edge stitch

Head

1 Cast on 40 stitches, 12/12/16.

2 Rib 3 rounds (bottom edge): knit 1, purl 1.

3 Knit 24 rounds.

4 End off with 2 stitches between decreasing. (See page 106.)

Body

1 Cast on 40 stitches, 12/12/16.

2 Rib 3 rounds (top edge): knit 1, purl 1.

3 Knit 40 rounds.

4 End off with 2 stitches between decreasing.

Small doll knitted by Katherine M., age 12

113

Arms

1 Cast on 15 stitches, 6/6/3.

2 Knit 40 rounds.

3 End off with 1 stitch between de-creasing.

Legs

Row knitting. Use the same two needles throughout.

1 Cast on 18 stitches.

2‡ Work 49 rows of stocking stitch. Finish knitting on an inside row.

3‡ Knit 9 stitches, cast in 6 stitches onto the right-hand needle (for the foot), hold the rest of the stitches on the left-hand needle without knitting them.

4‡ Knit 8 garter-stitch rows on the needle that has 15 stitches.

5‡ Cast off the 15 stitches.

6 Cast on 6 stitches onto the empty needle, then knit the 9 stitches you have been holding.

114

7‡ Knit 8 garter-stitch rows.

8‡ Cast off. Leave 1 arm's length of yarn for sewing.

FINISHING INSTRUCTIONS

Head and Body

1 Stuff the head firmly.

2 Thread the yarn left over from casting on into a tapestry needle. Weave the yarn through the loops around the open edge. See illustration. Pull the opening together tightly and fasten it with 2 tiny stitches across the hole.

3 Sew in all yarn ends.

4 Stuff the body to your liking. Close up the same way as the head (step 2).

Arms

1 Stuff.

2 Sew the opening together.

3 Wind a piece of yarn twice around the wrist tightly. Make a knot and sew the ends into the arm.

Legs

1 Sew foot together.

2 Stuff.

3 Sew up leg and stuff.

Joints

1 Sew head and arms to the body.

2 Sew the legs to the body while the doll is in a sitting position.

Hair

1 Choose yarn of the hair colour you want and cut about 80 strands that are double the hair-length desired.

2 Fold each strand in half and loop it through the top of the head the way you attach fringe (see page 44). Or, instead of fringe, you can glue a piece of fur to the head.

Face

If you like to imagine a face showing different moods, embroider eyes only. If the doll is for a very young child, it is better to show all features: eyes, nose, and mouth.

Double-Knitting-Yarn Doll

Sasha C., age 12

MATERIAL NEEDED

Three 25-gram balls of double-knitting yarn
1 set of 4 double-pointed knitting-needles, size 9 (See page 7.)
Stuffing material (See page 54.)
1 tapestry needle

WORK METHOD AND PATTERN STITCH

See fine-yarn doll.

KNITTING INSTRUCTIONS

‡Edge stitch

Head

1 Cast on 36 stitches, 12/12/12.

2 Rib 3 rounds (bottom edge): knit 1, purl 1.

3 Knit 17 rounds.

4 End off with 2 stitches between decreasing. (See page 106.)

115

Body

1 Cast on 36 stitches, 12/12/12.

2 Rib 3 rounds, knit 1, purl 1.

3 Knit 28 rounds.

4 End off with 2 stitches between de-decreasing.

Arms

Row knitting

1 Cast on 12 stitches.

2‡ Work 31 rows of stocking stitch.

3 Knit together 2 stitches for the entire row. Cut the yarn leaving 20 cm. Using a tapestry needle draw the yarn through the stitches. See illustration on page 114. Remove the knitting needle and pull the stitches together tightly.

Legs

Row knitting. Use the same two needles throughout.

1 Cast on 14 stitches.

2‡ Work 33 rows of stocking stitch. Finish knitting on an inside row.

3‡ Knit 7 stitches. Cast *in* 5 stitches onto the right-hand needle (for the foot), hold the rest of the stitches on the left-hand needle without knitting them.

4‡ Knit 5 garter-stitch rows on the needle that has 12 stitches.

5‡ Cast off the 12 stitches.

6 Cast on 5 stitches onto the empty needle, then knit the 7 stitches you have been holding.

7‡ Knit 5 garter-stitch rows.

8‡ Cast off. Leave 1 arm's length of yarn for sewing.

FINISHING INSTRUCTIONS

Same as for fine-yarn doll. (See page 114.)

HEAVILY TEXTURED PATTERNS FOR ROW KNITTING

‡Edge stitch

The following patterns cannot be indicated on diagrams. To try out the patterns, cast on 16 stitches. Make sure you knit each pattern row on the side of the work indicated. You may want to vary the patterns by knitting rows of stocking stitch between patterns.

PATTERN A

Cast on an even number of stitches.
First row (outside): ‡knit all stitches.
Second row (inside): ‡yarn-over, knit 2, then bring the yarn-over over the 2 knitted stitches and slide it off the needle. Repeat this sequence to end of row.

Third row: ‡knit all stitches.
Fourth row: ‡purl all stitches.
Repeat rows 1 to 4.

Knitted by Nancy H., age 14

PATTERN B

(This pattern has a tendency to stretch horizontally, so be careful to check the tension of your work. The knitting looks the same on both sides, making it ideal for a wrap around scarf. It is also ideal for a warm, bulky ski sweater.)

Cast on an even number of stitches.
First row (inside): ‡knit 1 stitch, then bring the yarn in front of the left-hand needle and slip the yarn and the next stitch as if to purl, over onto the right-hand needle.
Repeat this sequence to end of row.

Second row (outside): ‡knit together the yarn-over and the slipped stitch, then bring yarn in front of the left-hand needle and slip the yarn and the next stitch as if to purl, over onto the right-hand needle. Repeat this sequence to end of row.

Repeat the second row for all following rows.

Note: The pattern will not begin to appear until you have knitted several rows.

PATTERN C

Cast on an even number of stitches.
First row (outside): ‡knit all stitches.
Second row (inside): ‡knit 1 stitch, then bring the yarn in front of the left-hand needle and slip the next stitch as if to purl, dropping the yarn across the front of the stitch. Repeat this sequence to end of row.

Repeat rows 1 and 2.

PATTERN D

(This kind of knitting is called Tunisian Stitch; it is very solid and heavy. The structure of the knitted stitches lends itself to cross-stitch embroidery.) (See page 144.)

Cast on any number of stitches.

First row (inside): ‡Bring the yarn in front of the left-hand needle and slip the yarn and the next stitch as if to purl over onto the right-hand needle. Again bring the yarn in front of the left-hand needle and slip it together with the next stitch as if to purl over onto the right-hand needle.

Repeat to end of row.

Second row (outside): ‡knit together the yarn-over and the slipped stitch *through the back;* this will give it a twist. Repeat to end of row.

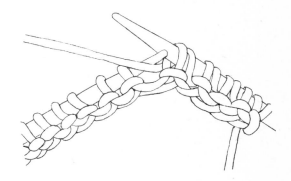

Repeat rows 1 and 2.

Serena R., age 12

119

HOW TO DESIGN AND KNIT CABLE PATTERNS

Cable patterns have a rope-like appearance with 2 'strands' inter-twining usually against a plain background. You have probably seen cabling on tennis and ski sweaters and socks.

DESIGNING CABLE PATTERNS

Your cable design may form a sort of ribbing pattern or the cabling may be treated as a dominant feature against a plain background of stocking stitch or purl stitches. To make your design you must decide on:

1 how many cables to have and how far apart they should be;

2 how wide each cable should be (generally, unless it is a special kind of cable, the width should never be more than 12 stitches and must always be an even number of stitches);

3 how many purl stitches to have bordering the cable;

4 how many straight rows to knit over each cable row (the row where you cross the strands). There should be at least as many rows knitted over the crossing or cable row as the number of stitches the cable is wide. The number of straight rows between cabling must always be uneven because you cable only on the outside rows.

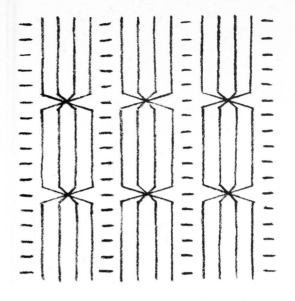

KNITTING INSTRUCTIONS

Outside Row

1 Work to the stitches you want to cable.

2 Put the first half of the stitches to be cabled onto an extra, double-pointed needle or wooden match. Leave these stitches to the back of the work if you want the cable to twist to the right, to the front if you want the cable to twist to the left. Knit the second half of the stitches.

3 Take the cable needle in your left hand and knit the stitches on the needle.

4 Resume regular knitting, cabling with the extra needle where planned.

Inside row

Purl over all purl stitches and knit over all knit stitches.

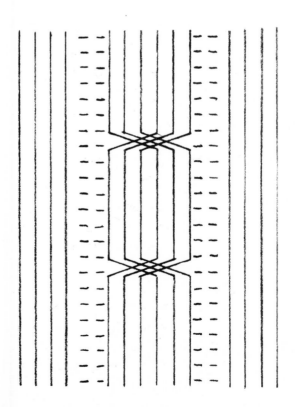

BABY PULLOVER: 8 TO 12 MONTHS

This raglan-sleeve pullover knits quite quickly. You may want to make several of them in different colours, yarn textures and pattern stitches. It fits loosely and it will take a long time for a child to grow out of it.

MATERIAL NEEDED

Five 25-gram balls of 4 ply yarn
1 pair of short knitting-needles, size 11
A drawstring made of yarn

WORK METHOD

Casting on
Row knitting
Edge stitch
Decreasing by knitting together stitches
Eyelet holes (See page 102.)
Casting off

PATTERN STITCH

Garter stitch, or choose your own

*Knitted for her niece
by Alexandra D., age 15*

KNITTING INSTRUCTIONS

The pullover is knitted in 4 parts: back, front and two sleeves. You may want to knit all ribbing on smaller needles for a tighter fit. (See page 75.)
‡Edge stitch.

Back

1   Cast on 82 stitches.

2‡ Rib 3·5 cm: knit 1, purl 1.

3‡ Work 15 cm in your pattern stitch.

4‡ Decrease for raglan shaping: knit together the last 2 stitches on every row until you have 58 stitches left on the needle.

5‡ Knit 1 row.

6‡ Rib 6·5 cm: start ribbing with a purl stitch. Finish on an inside row.

7‡ Work 1 row of eyelet holes: knit together 2 stitches, yarn-over. Repeat along the row.

8‡ Purl 1 row.

9‡ Cast off. Leave 1 arm's length of yarn for sewing.

Front

Work the same as back.

Sleeve

1   Cast on 54 stitches.

2‡ Rib 6·5 cm: knit 1, purl 1.

3‡ Work 15 cm of your pattern stitch.

4‡ Decrease for raglan shaping: knit together the last 2 stitches on every row until you have 30 stitches left on the needle.

5‡ Knit 1 row.

6‡ Rib, matching the front and back of the pullover. Start ribbing with a purl stitch. Finish on an inside row.

7‡ Work 1 row of eyelet holes: knit together 2 stitches, yarn-over. Repeat along the row.

8‡ Purl 1 row.

9‡ Cast off. Leave 1 arm's length of yarn for sewing.

FINISHING INSTRUCTIONS

1   Sew the pullover together on the inside. Overcast together all ribbing borders. Sew together the rest of the pullover with backstitches alongside the edge-stitched edges.

2   Weave the tie string through the eyelet holes.

Beth P., age 11

123

Knitted by Sita S., age 17

124

RAGLAN SLEEVE PULLOVER

This pullover can be knitted to any size and will look well on a boy or girl, man or woman. It has a round neck which can become a turtle-neck by knitting more ribbing.

MATERIAL NEEDED

Use any kind of yarn you want. Ask shop assistant about quantity
1 pair of knitting-needles (Size depends on yarn chosen. See chart on page 7.)
Knitting model (a sweater of the right size)

WORK METHOD

Row knitting
Edge stitch
Decreasing by knitting together stitches
Casting off

PATTERN STITCH

Ribbing
Stocking stitch, or choose your own pattern stitch

First knit a tension sample. See how many times the width of the sample will fit across the model sweater from armpit to armpit. Multiply the number of stitches in the sample by the number of times the sample fits across the model. See drawing. This will give you the number of stitches to cast on for the back or the front (they are the same). Add or subtract a few stitches to adjust to the exact size. Measure with your sample around the sleeve of the model just above the wrist for the number of stitches to cast on for the sleeve.

KNITTING INSTRUCTIONS

‡Edge stitch

This pullover is knitted in 4 separate parts: back, front, and 2 sleeves.

Back

1 Cast on required number of stitches.

2‡ Rib border to desired length.

3‡ Work in stocking stitch or knit your own pattern stitch straight up to the armpit. Compare length with model pullover.

4‡ Decrease for raglan shaping: knit together the last 2 stitches on every row. Stop decreasing 2·5 cm below the neckline of the model or when you have about 30 stitches left. Finish knitting on an inside row.

5‡ Knit 1 row.

6‡ Rib about 1·3 cm for a round neck, and about 15 cm if you want to make a turtle-neck.

7‡ Cast off in the ribbing pattern. Leave 1 arm's length of yarn for sewing.

Front

Work the same as back.

Sleeve

1 Cast on required number of stitches.

2‡ Rib border to the desired length.

3 Increase: knit 2 stitches out of the first and last stitches on the outside row, knitting your pattern in between. (See page 82.)

4 Count the decrease stitches on the back along one side of the raglan shaping. See drawing. Multiply this number by 2 and add 20. This is the total number of stitches the sleeve must be increased to. Half the stitches will be added on each side of the sleeve.

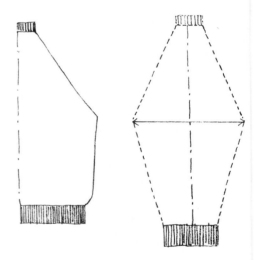

5 Measure the sleeve of the model from above the cuff to the armpit. Space the increasing rows evenly in between.

6‡ Knit the sleeve to the armpit, adding stitches as instructed in step 3.

7‡ Decrease for raglan shaping: knit together the last 2 stitches on every row. Stop decreasing when you have 20 stitches left. Finish on an inside row.

8‡ Knit 1 row.

9‡ Rib, matching the front and back.

10‡ Cast off in the ribbing pattern. Leave 1 arm's length of yarn for sewing.

FINISHING INSTRUCTIONS

Sew the pullover together on the inside. Overcast together all ribbing borders. Sew together the rest of the pullover with backstitches along the edge stitches.

RAGLAN SLEEVE CARDIGAN

The only difference between a raglan sleeve cardigan and a raglan sleeve pullover is the front. The front of a cardigan is divided in half like a jacket. Otherwise the knitting instructions are the same as for a pullover. You use the same materials and work methods for each.

KNITTING INSTRUCTIONS

Back and Sleeves

Follow instructions for raglan sleeve pullover. (See opposite.)

127

Front, Left Half

Cast on half the number of stitches used for the back, plus 4. The *first* 8 stitches of the first row are the border stitches. Knit these 8 stitches in garter rows or ribbing all the way up. See photograph.

Front, Right Half

Cast on the same number of stitches as you did for the left half. Use the *last* 8 stitches in the first row for the border. Make the first buttonhole when the knitting measures 2·5 cm. (See this page for how to knit a buttonhole.) Start each hole in the centre of the border and on an outside row. Cast off from 2 to 4 stitches depending on the size of the button you plan to use. In the following row cast back in as many stitches as you cast off. See photograph. Space the buttonholes about 5 cm apart.

FINISHING INSTRUCTIONS

Lay the border with the buttonholes over the opposite border. Mark with pins through the holes where the buttons go, centred in the border. Sew on the buttons with fine, matching cotton thread. Use the thread doubled. See raglan sleeve pullover for remaining finishing instructions.

128

How to Make a Buttonhole

To make a buttonhole, 2 rows of knitting are needed. Starting on an outside row, work to the place where the buttonhole should begin. Cast off as many stitches as you want the buttonhole to be long. Finish the row.

On the next (inside) row knit to the beginning of the buttonhole. Cast back *in* as many stitches as you cast off in the row before.

PROJECT 29

MATCHBOX CRADLE

Eliza B., age 13

While making this little cradle you will also be learning how to knit the heel of a sock.

MATERIAL NEEDED

Leftover 2, 3 or 4 ply yarn
1 set of five double-pointed knitting-needles, size 11
The bottoms of 2 matchboxes, about 4 cm × 5 cm

WORK METHOD

Round knitting
Row knitting
Decreasing with a slip stitch
Decreasing by purling together stitches
Picking up stitches
Casting off

PATTERN STITCH

Ribbing
Stocking stitch

KNITTING INSTRUCTIONS

Sides of Cradle

1 Cast on 40 stitches onto 4 needles, 10/10/10/10.

2 Rib 4 rounds: knit 1, purl 1.

3 On the next round continue to rib on the first, second and third needles. Knit all stitches on the fourth needle.

Back of Cradle

1 Set aside the empty needle. With the fourth needle, knit to the last stitch on the first needle; slip the last stitch as if to purl. See illustration. From now on work only on the needle with the most stitches.

2 Turn the knitting around to the inside (purl stitches). Knit the first 2 stitches, then purl until there are 2 stitches left on the needle. Knit 1 and slip as if to purl the last one.

3 Turn the knitting around to the outside (knit stitches). Knit all but the last stitch on the needle; slip as if to purl the last one.

4 Turn the knitting around to the inside. Repeat steps 2 and 3 until the straight-knitted part is about 2·5 cm long.

5 Look at your knitting. You will see purl stitches forming along each edge. Count these purl stitches on one side. Continue knitting as in steps 2 and 3 until there are 8 purl stitches along each edge. Finish knitting on an inside row.

Top of Cradle

1 Divide the 20 stitches on the needle into 2 equal parts. Mark the centre of each half with contrasting-coloured yarn.

2 Knit to 1 stitch before the second marker. Slip the stitch before the marker. Knit the stitch just after the marker and pull the slip stitch over the knitted stitch (similar to casting off). Turn the knitting around to the inside (purl stitches).

3 Slip the first stitch as if to purl. Purl to 1 stitch before the marker. Purl together the stitches before and after the marker. Turn the knitting around to the outside (knit stitches).

4 Slip the first stitch. Knit to 1 stitch before the gap that has appeared on the needle. Slip the stitch before the gap. Knit the stitch after the gap and pull the slipped stitch over the knitted stitch. Turn to the inside.

5   Slip the first stitch as if to purl. Purl to 1 stitch before the gap. Purl together the stitches before and after the gap. Turn to the outside.

6   Repeat steps 4 and 5 until all stitches to the outside of the gaps have been decreased. Finish knitting on an inside row. Remove the markers.

3   Rib the stitches on the second and third needles onto 2 separate needles.

4   With the empty fifth needle pick up the 8 stitches along the other edge as in step 2. See illustration. Then knit to the end of the round. You should have 13 stitches on the fourth needle.

Roof and Sides of Cradle

1   Knit to the centre of the needle and mark the place with a piece of yarn. You will be round knitting again from this point on.

2   Using the empty needle, knit the stitches to the edge of the straight-knitted part. Pick up a stitch from each edge stitch onto the same needle, alongside the straight-knitted part (8 stitches). See illustration. You should now have 13 stitches on the first needle of the round.

5 Cast off all stitches on the next round loosely. Cast off the stitches on the second and third needles in the ribbing pattern.

6 Cut the yarn, leaving about 7·5 cm.

FINISHING INSTRUCTIONS

1 Sew in yarn ends. (See page 140.)

2 Fit around matchbox bottoms as shown in illustration.

SOCKS

Although the knitting instructions are for plain knitted socks, the steps are the same for fancier ones.

MATERIAL NEEDED

Ten 25-gram balls of 4 ply yarn (wool mixed with synthetic) for knee socks, a little less for men's socks
1 set of 5 double-pointed knitting needles, size 11

WORK METHOD

Round knitting
Row knitting for the heel
Decreasing with a slip stitch
Decreasing by purling together stitches
Picking up stitches
End-decreasing

PATTERN STITCH

Ribbing
Stocking stitch

KNITTING INSTRUCTIONS

Knit a tension sample on 20 stitches with the yarn and needles you are going to use for your socks. You will use the sample in working out the number of stitches to cast on.

Knitted by Swiss children, aged 9–10

133

Knee Socks

Capital letters, A, B, C, and D refer to drawing.

With a tape-measure or strip of paper, measure around the calf of the leg. Use the tension sample to find the number of stitches to cast on (the number should divide by 4).

1 Cast on the stitches equally onto 4 needles.

2 Knit 2·5 cm. (This part will be folded under to hold a garter.)

3 Purl 1 round B.

4 Knit 2·5 cm.

Leg

1 Knit from 3·5 to 10 cm. Try on. Knitting should reach to top of calf B–C.

2 From C to D you decrease to follow the shape of the calf. Mark the beginning of the round with a piece of yarn.

   a Knit the first stitch, purl together the second and third stitches, knit to the last 3 stitches on the round, purl together 2 and knit the last stitch. You have decreased 2 stitches.

   b Knit from 8 to 12 rounds (the longer the leg, the more rounds between decreasing).

   c Repeat steps a and b until you have decreased one-quarter of the stitches you had cast on.

   d Divide the stitches evenly among the 4 needles again. Try on the sock. If the knitting does not reach to the heel D, knit to that point.

Straight Part of Heel
(row knitting)

The heel is knitted back and forth with the stitches on the fourth and first needles. Set aside the empty needle.

1 With the fourth needle, knit to the last stitch on the first needle; slip as if to purl the last stitch. See illustration. From now on you knit only on the needle with the most stitches.

4 Turn to the inside. Repeat steps 2 and 3 until the heel is about 2·5 cm long.

5 Look at your knitting. You will see purl stitches forming along each edge. Count these purl stitches on one side. Continue knitting as in steps 2 and 3 until the number of purl stitches is half the number of stitches on the heel needle *less 2*. Finish knitting on an inside row.

2 Turn the knitting around to the inside (purl stitches). Knit the first 2 stitches, then purl until there are 2 stitches left on the needle. Knit 1 and slip as if to purl the last one.

3 Turn the knitting around to the outside (knit stitches). Knit all but the last stitch on the needle; slip as if to purl the last one.

Turning the Heel

1 Divide the stitches on the heel needle in half. Mark the centre of each half with contrasting yarn.

2 Knit to 1 stitch before the second marker. Slip the stitch before the marker. Knit the stitch just after the marker and pull the slipped stitch

over the knitted stitch (similar to casting off). Turn to the inside.

3 Slip as if to purl the first stitch. Purl to 1 stitch before the marker. Purl together the stitches before and after the marker. Turn to the outside.

4 Slip the first stitch. Knit to 1 stitch before the gap on the needle. Slip the stitch before the gap. Knit the stitch after the gap and pull the slipped stitch over the knitted stitch. Turn to the inside.

5 Slip as if to purl the first stitch. Purl to 1 stitch before the gap. Purl together the stitches before and after the gap. Turn to the outside.

6 Repeat steps 4 and 5 until all stitches to the outside of gaps have been decreased. Finish knitting on an inside row. Remove the markers.

136

Completing the Heel

1 Knit to the centre of the heel needle and mark the place with a piece of yarn. You will be round knitting again from this point on.

2 Using the empty needle, knit the stitches to the edge of the heel. Pick up a stitch from each edge stitch alongside the heel onto the same needle (as many as you have purl stitches along the edge). See illustration.

3 Knit the stitches on the second and third needles onto separate needles.

4 With the fifth needle pick up the same number of stitches along the other edge of the heel as in step 2. See illustration. Then knit to the end of the round.

3 Repeat steps 1 and 2 until you have the same number of stitches on the round as you did before you started the heel.

Straight Part of Foot

1 Knit until the knitting covers the small toe. Try on the sock occasionally to check length.

2 End-decrease: (follow the rule on page 106).

Allow 6·5 cm for 6-stitch end-decreasing.
Allow 5 cm for 5-stitch end-decreasing.
Allow 4 cm for 4-stitch end-decreasing.
Allow 2·5 cm for 3-stitch end-decreasing.

Instep

1 Knit 2 rounds.

2 Knit to the last 2 stitches on the first needle, purl together these 2 stitches. Knit the stitches on the second and third needles. Purl together the first 2 stitches on the fourth needle. Knit to the end of the round.

Jennifer M., age 10

137

Men's Socks

KNITTING INSTRUCTIONS

Border

1 Cast on required number of stitches. (See page 134.)

2 Knit a 5 cm border, A–B, in ribbing: either knit 1, purl 1; or knit 2, purl 2.

Leg

Knit about 20 cm to bottom of leg, C–D, either in stocking stitch or in the ribbing used in the border (or another pattern).

Heel, Foot, and Toe

Follow from straight part of heel under instructions for knee socks. (See page 135.)

Knitted for her father by Diana H., age 14

Short Socks

A
B
C

KNITTING INSTRUCTIONS

Border

1 Cast on required number of stitches for leg at height you wish socks to reach. (See page 134.)

2 Work a border 2·5 cm long in ribbing: knit 1, purl 1 (A–B).

Leg

Knit 7·5 or 10 cm to bottom of leg, C in either stocking stitch, ribbing or another pattern stitch.

Heel, Foot, and Toe

Follow from straight part of heel under instructions for knee socks. (See page 135.)

Knitted by Swiss children, aged 8–12

SEWING INSTRUCTIONS FOR FINISHING KNITTING

How to Sew in Yarn Ends

All yarn ends must be finished off properly. *Never* just cut them off. Choose from the following the way that is best for your project:

1 Sew yarn ends through the edge-stitched edge for about 3·5 cm.

2 Sew yarn ends through knitting of the same colour on the inside for about the length of the tapestry needle.

3 Undo the knot on the inside. Cross the 2 yarn ends and sew them through knitting of the same colour in opposite directions. Sew through stitches for about the length of the tapestry needle.

4 At the tip of a mitten or sock, or in the ribbing pattern, sew in yarn ends in the shape of the letter U. Leave a small loop at the curve to allow for stretching.

in the illustration. Be careful not to miss a loop.

How to Sew a Seam

You make a seam when you fold knitting in half and sew 2 edges together. You also make a seam when you sew together 2 separate knitted parts.

SEWING TOGETHER THE CAST-ON EDGE

Sew the first stitch through the small knot that you will find in the corner opposite the piece of yarn left over from casting on. Then overcast together the casting-on loops as shown

SEWING TOGETHER THE CAST-OFF EDGE

Overcast together the *outside half* of each chain stitch as illustrated. Be careful not to miss a chain stitch.

SEWING TOGETHER THE EDGE-STITCHED EDGE

Sew the first stitch through the small knot that you will find in the corner opposite the piece of yarn left over from casting on. Then overcast both sides by sewing through the knots at the end of each garter-stitch row. Be careful not to miss a row.

SEWING A SEAM IN STOCKING-STITCH AND OTHER PATTERNS

Turn the knitting inside out. Pin together the edges. With backstitches sew alongside the edge-stitched edge. (For

backstitch see page 144.) *Exception:* When the knitting is very narrow, like the arms and legs for a doll, it is difficult to turn it inside out after sewing. Therefore, overcast together the edge-stitched edges on the *outside*. See sewing together borders below.

SEWING TOGETHER BORDERS

Borders are usually knitted in the ribbing pattern. Sew them together through the edge stitches as shown in the illustration. This makes the seam look the same on each side, which is important if you plan to fold over the ribbing. Be careful on which side you sew in the yarn ends, so they will not show on the outside of the turned-up ribbing.

142

How to Sew Together Stuffed Parts

Pin the 2 parts together where you want to attach them. Then sew them together with small running-stitches, sewing 1 stitch in one part, the next stitch in the other part.

SEWING THE CAST-ON EDGE TO THE CAST-OFF EDGE

Thread the yarn end left for sewing. Sew the first stitch through the loop made by the last stitch you cast on. See illustration. Pick up the outside half of the chain stitches and the cast-on loops on the other side. Be careful not to miss a stitch on either side.

SEWING STITCHES YOU NEED TO KNOW

1 Running-Stitch

Worked from right to left.

2 Backstitch

Worked from right to left.

3 Cross-Stitch

Worked from right to left.

a Make first diagonal stitch from A to C.

b Make second diagonal stitch from D to B.

Note: The second diagonal stitch must always cross the first, facing in the same direction.

4 French knot

Used wherever needed.

5 Swiss darning stitch

This follows the line of the knitted stitch.

a Horizontally: work from right to left.

b Vertically: work from bottom to top.

Running Stitch

Backstitch

Cross-Stitch

French knot

Swiss darning stitch

INDEX

SURREY COUNTY LIBRARY

(Headquarters, 140 High Street, Esher) | JNF |

This book must be returned to the Branch or
Travelling Library from which it was borrowed, by the
latest date entered above.

Charges will be payable on books kept overdue.

TOKEN SECTION | Please note that reminders will not
be sent for books kept overdue.   L24